Treasures *of* HEAVEN

LESSONS FROM THE OTHER SIDE

CARI L. MURPHY

Bestselling Author of *Create Change Now*

BALBOA.
PRESS
A DIVISION OF HAY HOUSE

Balboa Press books may be ordered through booksellers or by contacting:

Balboa Press
A Division of Hay House
1663 Liberty Drive
Bloomington, IN 47403
www.balboapress.com
1 (877) 407-4847

Because of the dynamic nature of the Internet, any web addresses or links contained in this book may have changed since publication and may no longer be valid. The views expressed in this work are solely those of the author and do not necessarily reflect the views of the publisher, and the publisher hereby disclaims any responsibility for them.

The author of this book does not dispense medical advice or prescribe the use of any technique as a form of treatment for physical, emotional, or medical problems without the advice of a physician, either directly or indirectly. The intent of the author is only to offer information of a general nature to help you in your quest for emotional and spiritual well-being. In the event you use any of the information in this book for yourself, which is your constitutional right, the author and the publisher assume no responsibility for your actions.

Any people depicted in stock imagery provided by Thinkstock are models, and such images are being used for illustrative purposes only.
Certain stock imagery © Thinkstock.

Printed in the United States of America.

ISBN: 978-1-4525-8648-9 (sc)
ISBN: 978-1-4525-8649-6 (e)

Balboa Press rev. date: 12/6/2013

Dedication

To my precious daughter who shines the light of joy and remembrance into my life and heart on a daily basis, I love you eternally. You are my gift from heaven. You're my inspiration.

My infinite gratitude, respect and love to Tim for your unwavering support, insight, and of course, for all the laughter along the way. You've made the journey rewarding and worthwhile.

To my beautiful Mother, you GLOW like no other. You light up my life! You continually reveal the true meaning of love and acceptance. My gratitude for you is beyond description. My love for you beyond this world.

To my family...
thank you for being there. I always love coming "home."

To my clients, audiences, listeners, and readers,
I appreciate you more than you know.

To all the beautiful souls who have touched my heart and soul on this journey, I thank you. Your presence has provided me with the opportunity to see with new eyes, hear with new ears and feel with an ever-expanding heart. Thank you. Thank you. Thank you.

PRAISE FOR
TREASURES OF HEAVEN:
LESSONS FROM THE OTHER SIDE

"What if there are no victims? What if you are actually the creator of your life? Cari Murphy's new book addresses these questions and many more in a beautiful and unique way. This book is about empowering you to look at the world from a totally-different perspective, and *Cari is a master at inviting you to the possibilities that are truly available*, using her experience from 'beyond the veil."

> ~ **Dr. Dain Heer,** co-creator Access
> Consciousness, author *Being You,*
> *Changing the World* and *Embodiment:*
> *The Manual You Should Have Been*
> *Given When You Were Born*

"*Treasures of Heaven* is a **must have** if you truly want to change your life! Once again, Cari Murphy captures the essence of what it means to live a soulful life. She shares how her perspective expanded greatly after her near death experience and how it changed her life. Through her teaching and exercises she helps you learn how to live a harmonious, joyful life. She inspires and encourages while providing methods and exercises to enable you to *harmonize your body, mind and spirit*. She helps you to see how difficulties are opportunities and how to live your truth to reconnect with the heaven that is within you. *I highly recommend this enlightening book* to anyone who wants to live a more fulfilling life filled with love, happiness and success."

> ~ **Carol Whitaker**, Author, Speaker,
> Life Transformation Coach

"It has been said, "We are spiritual beings having a human experience." Cari Murphy reveals time and again how true this belief is. Throughout her most recent work, Treasures of Heaven; Lessons from the Other Side, **Cari masterfully shows the practical side of spirituality and how virtually anyone can have an incredible life journey. This book is a must read** for anyone who questions why you are here, those who have been on a spiritual quest for years and those who are just beginning to understand you truly are a spiritual being having a human experience."

~ **Kathleen Gage**, Author, Speaker,
Visibility Business Consultant

"Current evidence strongly points to a dimension of our mind that is infinite in space and time, therefore immortal, eternal, and one with all other minds. Cari Murphy's powerful new book opens the door to this domain and leads us to this awareness. If you are looking for greater joy and fulfillment in your life, *don't deny yourself this journey."*

~ **Larry Dossey, MD** author of *ONE MIND: How Our Individual Mind Is Part of a Greater Consciousness and Why It Matters*

"Cari's latest book offers *empowering and essential insights* to remind us of our eternal nature and our power and birthright to live heaven on earth!"

~ **Colette Baron Reid,** Bestselling Author,
Motivational speaker & Internationally
Renowned Intuitive Counselor

"Cari's book, Treasures of Heaven, will inspire you on your journey of self-discovery. If you are looking for heightened awareness and to reach your true potential, *I highly suggest you read this book!"*

~ **Dr. Steve G. Jones**, Ed.D.
Clinical Hypnotherapist

"Read this book to awaken your heart, mind, and spirit! I loved it!"

~ **Dr. Joe Vitale,** author "The
Attractor Factor" and "At Zero"

"*You will love this book!* As you read *TREASURES OF HEAVEN: LESSONS FROM THE OTHER SIDE*, you will be taken into a journey of possibilities. *This is a book you won't want to put down* – each page filled with layers of insight and knowledge. Easy to read and filled with nuggets of wisdom to open your heart and mind. Get ready to discover the answers to your greatest challenges so you will release the fear, worry and anxiety keeping you from the life you desire. In a nutshell, *Cari Murphy has done it again!*"

~ **Dr. Fabrizio Mancini,** International
Bestselling Author of *The Power of Self-Healing*
and President Emeritus of Parker University

"You will remember your power, purpose and potential more fully than ever after reading this transformational book! The divinely inspired insights are profound, yet practical. Give yourself the gift of igniting your light. *Cari reminds us of our birthright – to create heaven on earth.*"

~ **Sunny Dawn Johnston**, Inspirational
Speaker, Spiritual Teacher, and Author of
*Invoking the Archangels - A Nine-Step Process
to Heal Your Body, Mind and Soul*

"*Treasures of Heaven* weaves masterfully profound wisdom and practical tools into a tapestry of hope and empowerment. With great clarity and compassion, Cari takes you on a transformational journey that expands your consciousness, lightens your heart, and enhances your ability to tap into your infinite potential. If you are ready to uplevel your life – *this is a must-read!*"

~ **Dr. Friedemann Schaub, MD, PhD,
author of The Fear and Anxiety Solution**

"Cari is the rare real deal! I've had first-hand experience with her work on a personal and professional level on numerous occasions throughout the years. *I promise you will not be disappointed in getting* **great life-changing results!** *Read this book!*

~ **Deb Scott, BA, CPC**
Award Winning Author:
The Sky is Green & The Grass is Blue
Award Winning Radio Host:
The Best People We Know Show

"Soul enriching! In her latest book, *Treasures of Heaven*, Cari expertly *weaves the mystical and the practical* while lovingly guiding readers in remembering the truth of who they are – expansive beings of love and light who hold the power to transform their inner and outer lives."

~ **Linda Joy**, Publisher of Aspire Magazine,
Host of Inspired Living Secrets

"In her powerful new book, Treasures of Heaven, Cari Murphy combines her talents as a Soul Success Coach with the knowledge she gained through her near death experience. Through these pages, Cari will give you the opportunity to **bring the truth, wisdom and power of your eternal self into the present moment.**»

~ **Dr. Annie Kagan,** Author of the Bestsellling
Book, The Afterlife of Billy Fingers

"I had the honor of being the very first guest on Cari Murphy's wonderful radio program in January of 2009. Since then, I've watched her expand her audience and **touch countless lives around the world.** In her latest book, Cari reveals her experience of heaven and shares practical tools you can use to create heaven here on Earth. *A must read!*"

~ **Noah St. John,** author *The Book of
Afformations®: Discovering The Missing Piece to
Abundant Health, Wealth, Love, and Happiness*

"I love this book!!! Cari Murphy's new book is the perfect guide filled with potent wisdom for transforming your body, mind and soul for greater fulfillment and inner peace. It's *filled with lots of juicy exercises and powerful tips* you'll use again and again. *Study this book. It's truly magnificent!"*

~ **Mary Allen**, America's Inner Peace Coach
and Author of *The Power of Inner Choice*

"Cari's latest book, TREASURES OF HEAVEN: LESSONS FROM THE OTHER SIDE, is both *wise and wonderful!* It opens your heart as well as your soul with *practical wisdom* and advice. *Splendid book! Folks will get a lot of value out of this gem!"*

~ **Denise Linn**, *author of 17 books including the Bestsellers Sacred Space and Sacred Legacies*

~

In this groundbreaking new book, Best Selling Author, Soul Success Coach, and Award Winning Host of *"THE CARI MURPHY SHOW: STRAIGHT TALK FOR THE SOUL",* Cari Murphy invites you on a journey of self-discovery that will support you in creating "heaven on earth." *You are cordially invited to bring a NEW, highly expansive "you" into existence.* A pretty grand invitation? Yes, it is. The vastness of your soul is grander than anything in your wildest imagination. The authentic "you" came into this world ready to ignite the sparks of divinity within you, to experience the spiritual evolution which is your birthright. We are eternal beings of light with the spiritual power to shape our reality with conscious intentions. *Our future is not set in stone. We create it from moment to moment.*

Cari reminds us there are no accidents, only divinely designed opportunities placed in our paths during moments of greater awareness. Readers are empowered to take responsibility for their choices and liberate themselves from the illusion that they are victims of their circumstances. ***Cari reveals the insights, principles, and tools gained from her near death experience in 1997.*** These have transformed her life and the lives of clients, audiences, readers and listeners around the world.

Her messages are practical and uplifting, intended to accelerate your transformation and inspire you with new meaning, purpose and joy in your journey of expansion. With this fresh, broader perspective, you will hold the key to conscious creation and empowered living.

Each chapter offers clear action steps and exercises to integrate the messages in practical ways. You are guided toward creative control of your life experience and shown your potential for generating inner worth, outer wealth and vibrant health. You are encouraged to apply the information with inspired action to generate new opportunities and fulfilling outcomes in your day-to-day experiences.

This book will show you how to:

- ⅄ Move from Stressed to Blessed
- ⅄ Embrace Your Role as a Catalyst for Positive Change
- ⅄ Celebrate Life as the Grand and Glorious Adventure it should Be
- ⅄ Consciously Evolve Beyond Limitations to Embrace Infinite Possibilities
- ⅄ Learn the Importance of Daily Self Nurturing Practices
- ⅄ Explore New Territories of Consciousness, Awareness, and Love
- ⅄ Tap into Your Creative Potential
- ⅄ Generate Positive Momentum
- ⅄ Make Joy, Fun and Ease Daily Priorities
- ⅄ Clarify, Refine, and Simplify Your Desires
- ⅄ Turn Challenges into the Fuel for Your Expansion
- ⅄ Expand Your Approach to Personal and Professional Success

- ⅄ Enhance the Quality of your Health, Wealth and Relationships
- ⅄ Shift from Dull, Uninspired, Auto-Pilot Living into Purposeful Living

This transformational book will change the way you approach life. It will open doors to new possibilities that align with the dreams and desires of your soul. By expanding your perspective, you will unleash a flood of beauty, love, abundance and prosperity.

New opportunities wait just beyond the confines of the old, boxed-in expectations you had for yourself and your life. *Open your heart, mind, body and spirit to this dynamic windfall of opportunities.* Align yourself with the brilliant light and infinite nature of your soul as life begins opening up in novel and magical ways. **Give yourself the gift of renewed exhilaration for life! You deserve this. Now is the time to claim it!**

CONTENTS

Prologue: Beyond the Body: The Day I Left the World Behind   xvii
Introduction: Turning Points   xxvii

PART I EXPANDING PERSPECTIVE   1

1. Infinite Possibilities   1
2. Challenges Are Opportunities   6
3. Lifting the Veil   11
4. Soul Success   19
5. Accountability   23
6. Transcending Limits   31
7. Transcending Attachments   39
8. Inner Worth and Outer Wealth   44
9. Seize the Moment   50

PART II CONSCIOUS LIVING   59

10. What Is Synchronicity?   59
11. Awareness   73
12. Inner Compass   82
13. Your Vibrational Frequency   89
14. Unique Soul Signature   96
15. Feminine and Masculine Energies   101
16. Evolving by Choice   109
17. The Blueprint of Your Divine Destiny   117
18. Destiny and Free Will   122
19. Being "Spiritual"   126

PART III SOUL-DRIVEN SUCCESS 131

20. Soul Driven Goals   131
21. Flexibility   135
22. Empowering Vocabulary   142
23. Create Wellness (It's an Inside Job!)   147
24. Sacred Geometry   156
25. Elixir of Eternal Youth   165
26. Thrive   174
27. Bridging Heaven and Earth   181
28. Generating Momentum   189
29. From Stressed to Blessed   195
30. Enjoy the Ride   201

Prologue

BEYOND THE BODY:
THE DAY I LEFT THE WORLD BEHIND

Language is so limiting, but I'll do my best to convey my 1997 experience when I entered a dimension many call "Heaven" and returned forever changed. Some of my memories have vanished, but many are vivid because they transformed my life. My entire perspective on life shifted radically.

It was November, almost Thanksgiving. I'd had a high fever for weeks, so my sweet husband (unbeknownst to me) flew my mother into town to convince me to see a doctor. She insisted I see a special-ist to figure out what was happening with my body. I never liked going to the doctor and I thought I could wait the fever out. I was strong willed, so telling me what to do didn't usually go over well, but I finally relented, and Mom and I made our way to the Houston Diagnostic Clinic. The Houston Medical Center is world-renowned, so we arrived with high hopes of finding answers. I underwent a battery of tests that day, continuing to feel feverish and weak.

The day seemed so long. I was exhausted, and tired of being poked, examined and tested for hours on end. At some point, I recall sitting in one of those cubicles having my blood drawn. My beautiful, sweet, loving Mom was standing close by, and I remember doctors, nurses and technicians moving all around. I was trying to remain brave, but I had always been afraid of needles. I had to imagine my precious two year old daughter sitting right beside me, keeping me confident, fearless and grounded. I imagined showing her there was nothing to fear from doctors or needles. But as much as I tried to hold those thoughts and images, they were slipping away. I was suddenly clearly aware that I was disconnecting from my physical body and began to slump down, as I struggled to stay in my body.

But the connection was slipping and I was
losing consciousness as "Cari."
Finally, I surrendered. I felt myself flow out of my body
as my mother screamed
"Please help my daughter... I think she's dying!"
Then everything faded into the silence.

First I saw bright flashes of light, then glimpses of my life from the time I was born, the defining moments that had changed my life's direction or impacted me greatly. I also saw seemingly unimportant experiences as I watched this movie of my life reveal the highlights, low points, challenges, and so many of the simple moments of my life.

The experiences flashed before me until reaching the present day, and then came the brightest, most all encompassing light I could imagine. It surrounded me and permeated me. I was not separate from it.

And then...it was over. I opened my eyes, saw I was crumpled on the floor with doctors and nurses surrounding me. Everyone was talking at once as my precious mother cried. Their fear was palpable, but at this point, it becomes a little fuzzy again.

I'm told I was placed on a gurney and taken to a private room to be monitored. I was trying to process what had happened to me, knowing something very important had taken place, something I couldn't explain logically or put into words. I was afraid to speak about it for fear of others' judgment or misunderstanding. I couldn't comprehend what had taken place myself, but I was different. Something extraordinary had happened.

I stayed silent, lost in an inner world of wonder, fascination and awe. "Did that really happen?" I wondered to myself.

I didn't share that brief journey into the light with my Mom or my husband. My Mom has always been the greatest supporter and cheerleader in my life, but I couldn't tell her. Looking back, we were both bewildered and shocked. Mom later told me she didn't want to scare me (or my husband) by letting us know she thought I had died... so we both simply internalized the experience for many years.

When I was allowed to go home, I was told to rest in bed for many weeks, which seemed like an eternity to an active person like me. The "diagnosis" was a heart condition that had been unnoticed and untreated for years, so I was put on medication to stabilize my blood pressure. The severity of the heart condition came as quite a surprise (even though I was diagnosed with having a heart murmur as a child) because I was in excellent physical condition. I was certified as a physical trainer and wrote fitness articles for magazines at the time. Yet, this was the diagnosis, and I needed to let my body recover by limiting activity and remaining in bed for what seemed like a very, very long time.

I never spoke to my husband about the experience. He was very supportive and took great care of both our daughter and me during that time. I cocooned myself in a bliss bubble to which only I had access! I spent the next six weeks in bed in a newly expansive state of "being."

Something powerful and beautiful had happened
during my time "away" from my body:
a portal to my soul had opened,
allowing me to re-member things I didn't know I knew!

During those weeks, I had an insatiable desire to read books on near death experiences, soul energy, consciousness and healing. I became a spiritual sponge. I was ready to understand what had happened to me, and to meet others who had experienced something similar. I began doing a great deal of writing. I had been a writer prior to this experience and had even published my first book about a year earlier in the genre of psychology and relationships.

But this was different. Very different. The insights and concepts flowing into me were entirely new, and the words streaming out were coming from a new "Cari." These insights seemed new and familiar at the same time, knowing at my core they were all true. I was surprised by the insights coming to me, and thought, "I didn't know I knew all of this!" Yet I understood that a deeper part of me did know it.

I was simply re-membering what I already knew.

My perspective was changing with each new day and brought new awakenings that seemed so completely real and natural. I allowed it all to flow through me. I was writing in depth about chakras, auras, soul energy, and key human life lessons in ways that surprised and delighted me at the same time. I didn't learn any of this in school. The information was coming from within, from a broader, fuller part of me. It was coming from my soul, from my expansive, infinite self. I now had access to it all.

Weeks went by and I still hadn't told anyone about the experience of leaving my body. I didn't think anyone would understand and I didn't want to be ridiculed or judged. I was happy just living in this new expansive state, and appreciating the portal which had opened between my human self and my infinite self. My writing during that time was eventually published in 2001 in *YOUR SOUL IS CALLING: WILL YOU ACCEPT THE CALL?* Looking back, I don't think many people were open to the concepts and ideas in that book. All these years later, many still consider the concepts "out there!" But many others remember or wish to remember our vast potential beyond this physical realm. Many yearn for these truths at a deeper level, truths which remind us of who we really are beyond the limitations of this physical world. These truths touch a deep chord inside because they reveal the vast storehouse of knowledge within our infinite selves.

*We are so much more than the physical body,
so much more than we remember.*

We are infinite beings, and this lifetime is just one experience in the vast journey of our souls. We hold within us all the knowledge, light, and wisdom to heal or create whatever we wish. This might sound impossible or even silly, but I will show you it is more tangible and practical than anything else I've ever learned.

Many years have passed since that transformational experience in 1997. My mother and I didn't speak about that day until years later, when I began to write about it and discuss it publicly. For a long time, I quietly experienced my expansion, trusting the new energy as my journey unfolded. I'm sure those around me noticed the changes, as I shifted out of old friendships and relationships and into new ones. I became much more secure and independent, no longer needing outside validation. I no longer feared being different, or felt the need to follow the crowd. I embraced my uniqueness and relished the opportunity to be a pioneer, with progressive ideas about life, love and our universe.

New people, experiences and opportunities seemed to magically enter my life with effortless grace and ease. The majority of the souls who were drawn into my experience were people with whom I felt an immediate sense of connection. I knew in my soul that we already knew one another before this life, outside of physical constraints. I knew we had "planned" to meet here during the "pre-planning" phases our souls go through prior to entering each lifetime.

*I was fascinated and empowered
as I remembered I had chosen my parents, husband, and daughter,
as well as the biggest challenges, struggles and life lessons
I needed to face in this particular lifetime.*

I saw things from a broader perspective, saw the overriding need for new levels of compassion, forgiveness, healing and love in all areas of my life. I stopped sweating the "small" stuff! I released a great deal of guilt, resentment, shame, fear and judgment, and brought more harmony and peace into my life. It hurt to say goodbye to old comfortable routines, but I wanted to keep expanding. I wanted to fly.

Options and information continued to flood my awareness and my world. I felt a sense of love for all people which confused me because I previously had somewhat inflexible ideas about life and love.

The information from my soul continues to be revealed in layers. The more I remember, the more I realize there is to remember! That day in the diagnostic hospital opened the door to my infinite essence, and new doors have consistently been made available to me since. It will always be my choice to walk through those new doors of opportunity and love. Expansion never ends and I wake each day wondering what opportunities and adventures are in store for me. I make a daily decision to move through my journey with a sense of positive expectancy.

I still don't completely understand all of the concepts and information revealed to me because my human brain can't comprehend it all. And yet, my soul knows the truth.

I was given this gift of expanded awareness
to impact not only my journey in life,
but to share this information with anyone
open to receiving it.

It hasn't always been easy. I am still challenged, but I have learned to flow through these experiences with as little resistance and as much grace as possible, knowing my foundation is secure. I now know all is well all the time, even amidst the most challenging times.

Since returning to my body, I have felt surrounded and embraced by divine love. I am always surrounded by a "team of light" in the higher realms, who are with me and available to support me every moment. Each one of us has this divine support system, but many haven't realized it yet.

I have devoted many years to sharing my insights with readers, clients, and audiences, striving to remind others of their own power to consciously create their lives. I am so grateful for the opportunity to share these truths.

> *I now clearly understand that we are the only ones who create our lives. We are solely responsible and accountable for the quality of our existence.*

We are the only ones who matter in judging ourselves over what we've "accomplished". We are extensions of God, not separate from God as my childhood religion suggested.

I was raised a Christian. My family attended the Methodist Church each week and I went to Catholic school. Religion was deeply ingrained in me, but it was confusing to see the doctrinal differences between those two Christian religions, each believing their way was right or best. I experienced some very joyful times in a church setting, but even then I felt the "truths" revealed by the church weren't the full truths. I knew in the depths of my heart that God doesn't judge or punish or feel disappointment and anger about my choices. He isn't even a "He" or a "Man sitting in the Sky!"

Humans created religions. I knew God didn't create one religion to be superior to all others. Looking back on my religious upbringing, I gained a great deal from the people, surroundings, and lessons made available my family and me. Religion keeps many individuals and families grounded and connected in a world can be so alienating and chaotic at times. But now I have expanded my belief about religion to allow for all the roads that lead to God. No organized religion is better or worse than another, because they all hold the same primary truths.

I respect and honor every person's decision about how they wish to experience their own growth and expansion. *We each have our own journeys, and our own stories to write.* So I don't cling to any particular dogma. I simply pay attention to my own journey – the only one I have any control over!

I hope this book and its messages will serve as a reminder for you. If the information resonates within you, it's because your soul already knows it to be true. It is a truth free of judgments and guilt. Now is the time to awaken and remember your authentic power. You can choose to let go of anything that restrains you in your journey, and step into your wholeness. Claim your birthright to design your own destiny!

There is truly no right or wrong way to do go through life. Ingrained but unquestioned beliefs about ourselves and the world around us make us judgmental. Spiritual expansion requires us to have the courage to move beyond our limited thinking, and out of our comfort zones. Beliefs from our past, based on our religions or cultures, must be critically questioned. The beauty of free will is our ability to choose what to keep and what to let go of. We decide to live the illusion of a safely protected reality, where external information is judged, ridiculed and feared – OR, we choose to walk through and beyond the self-generated barriers which have prevented us from experiencing the fullness and wholeness of our lives.

We are so much more than religion leads us to believe. I'm grateful for the empowering tools I gained from my religious upbringing, thankful for so many beautiful experiences with my family and congregation. But, I am far more liberated as an adult, knowing that spirituality is much broader than religion. Spiritual awareness allows for true compassion, forgiveness, acceptance, tolerance and love, beyond the boundaries of dogma.

My greatest hope is that you will re-member
just how innately powerful, brilliant and beautiful you are.

The human experience is merely one facet your multidimensional, eternal soul. You chose this physical body for the immense gift it offers: the wonderful opportunity to experience separation from the eternal and divine. Our souls choose to experience this life, knowing we will be temporarily separated from the light and love of the unifying cosmic realm.

We are born, and forget we are part of the divine.
The beauty of our earthly experience is remembering.

We are intended to expand, thrive and realize our infinite potential in this world. Our greatest challenge is overcoming the limitations of having forgotten our divinity. We must re-member our infinite capacity for creating our lives in whatever ways we choose, to support our expansion and the expansion of everyone else on the planet.

May each word in this book remind you of what you already know. May you begin to celebrate yourself as the courageous, magnificent soul you are. This is your birthright.

And now... a deep breath. The remainder of the book will reveal the insights I've gained since my near death experience. I will relay the most empowering messages that have come through me, the ones that continue to support me in my own day-to-day expansion. May they also support you in yours.

Introduction

TURNING POINTS

We encounter turning points in our journeys which offer growth and expansion through revolutionary opportunities. These are ***"divinely designed options," allowing us to renew, reshape, and expand our reality*** beyond any limiting ways of the past. We have the ability to shift from dull, uninspired, auto-pilot living into purposeful living! These turning points offer the option to create powerful and positive shifts within and around us, shining light into the expansiveness of our tomorrows.

As we shift within, the outer world also shifts.

The external world is simply a mirror reflecting back to us a physical representation of our existing beliefs and truths. ***The inner creates the outer.*** So, as we expand our beliefs to reflect the eternal nature of our souls, our physical reality mirrors that expansion. I hope this book and its insights offer you a very powerful, divinely designed opportunity to step into your innate divinity and greatness. What could be better than that?

Expanding your perspective on life is empowering and liberating, like putting on a new pair of glasses so everything around you becomes crystal clear. I wish to provide you with practical tools to access your infinite self. ***We are all infinite beings with unlimited power to design our destinies.*** Beyond the human brain, we carry the light-encoded information accumulated during a multitude of lifetimes here on earth and beyond. As eternal beings, we exist on many levels, aside from the physical plane. We have the capacity to design our expansion from moment to moment. We needn't wait for life to happen to us! Within us, we have all the answers and insights we could ever desire. This innate wisdom speaks to us through intuition and guides our journey. We must listen to, trust and act on this ever-present inner guidance.

We are powerful beyond measure, with potential we haven't even begun to tap. As you begin to trust the voice of your soul, your reality will realign with your newly expansive nature. Now is the time to experience the joy, magic, miracles and abundance you so richly deserve.

My insights are simple. ***Healing and expansion are always simple. We need not complicate the process!*** Believe that magic and miracles are not reserved for a special few. They are available to anyone. Refuse to limit what is possible!

It's time we had some fun with life and its time to lighten up – literally! I say that playfully AND respectfully. I know we all face deeply challenging times, but the way we approach these challenges will define our experience and determine the outcomes. I intend to share insights that will open new doors for you, doors of awareness which will allow you to expand beyond all limitations and generate revolutionary success in every facet of your life.

All doors have keys,
and the heavenly inspired keys offered in this book
produce soul-driven solutions which will make you a pioneer.

Remember, you already possess the tools and knowledge to guide you every step of the way. You have always been intended to be a pioneer in your own life, to explore new territories of consciousness, awareness, and love.

Your higher self will reach beyond your personality and physical body to draw this information into your experience. You will reclaim the divine, and remember your limitless nature. I hope this book becomes the catalyst for your growth and positive change. Spiritual expansion is a gift you give yourself, your loved ones and all humanity.

You are cordially invited to usher a NEW, highly expansive "you" into existence. A pretty grand invitation? Yes, it is. The vastness of your soul is grander than anything in your wildest imagination. The authentic "you" came into this world ready to ignite the sparks of divinity and grace within you, to experience the spiritual evolution which is your birthright.

There are no accidents.
Divinely designed opportunities are placed in our paths
during moments of greater awareness.

You will become more and more aware of these crucial turning points. These brilliantly designed opportunities to elevate your consciousness will happen with greater frequency as your awareness is heightened. You will shift into vibrant, intentional living. **Intentions are creative, setting wheels of energy into motion, making the universe more responsive to your requests.**

Choose an intention right now that reveals your soul's deepest hopes and desires and say it out-loud. **As you read this book, your intention will transform your reality.**

I am honored your soul has led you to this small book, and hope it becomes an opportunity to refine and enhance the overall quality of your life. It is my invitation to greater awareness, clarity, and love. **This is a time for celebration.** Learn to listen to the voice of your soul and take action to support your evolution.

We must choose to engage ourselves in the continuous emergence of this new reality. We have a personal responsibility as souls to embrace our authentic, innate power and raise our energy levels every day. *We have all been given a gift, a grand and glorious adventure for the soul.* It's time we claim it!

This book was written to be applied. The application of knowledge turns into wisdom. Let the information and insights keep you grounded, inspire new levels of awareness, increase the brilliance of your light, and remind you of the magnificent, limitless, eternal being you are. This book can be read in sequential order or randomly. *You may start where you wish. Simply open the book to a new page each day and find passages that will encourage divine guidance from your soul*.

As an awakened person leading with your soul, you will learn the importance of daily self nurturing practices. These consistent practices allow the wisdom you remembered on your journey to become animated, to project through your energy field in positive, empowering ways. Therefore, *I suggest reading a chapter each day as you develop a new self-nurturing process to become the creative designer of your life experience.* A daily practice which keeps your thoughts, feelings, words and actions aligned with your soul will create a more peaceful, harmonious and fulfilling lifestyle.

Our energy fields are made of light, and the projection of this light expands and amplifies your daily experiences. We all have the power to synchronize our energy to the vibration of love, joy, and abundance. *We achieve this with practice, awareness and daily commitment.* This will become a joyful practice, being consistently devoted to your own growth, healing and expansion.

We all need reminders of what we already know
in the deepest recesses of our being.
This book offers you those reminders.

To shift your perception, you must be committed to your evolution and experience it with a sense of joy and divine enthusiasm. The heaviness in our lives is a choice, but so is the lightness. *Why not adopt a play-full, light, and empowering routine which nourishes you each day with spiritual insights and reminders?* There is no downside here. This book and its messages offer you a divinely designed opportunity to experience more of your true self.

We are all divine expressions of God, playing our roles in the unfolding story of our universe. *We are intended to be deliberate creators of our experience.* So step into a fluid, open connection with your soul, and align your energy with your divine blueprint. You have one, whether you remember it or not.

We are all eternal beings of light with tremendous innate power. Remembering this allows us to *affect our reality with conscious intentions.* Our future is not set in stone. We create it from moment to moment. We consciously choose the type of energy we radiate into the world to illuminate each experience. This way of living empowers us from the inside-out. Choose to focus on inner and outer success, and step into the role of a true creator. You determine what you will attract and repel. This is where the magic happens and the fun begins! Acknowledge your divine role as a catalyst for change. You can begin now.

As you remember your creative power you will use it to shift from merely surviving in separation to thriving in wholeness and unity. You hold the power to be an empowering luminary, a pioneer of higher awareness. This role isn't reserved for a special few. It is available to us all. Our infinite souls hold divine light and the innate wisdom to provide daily insights and guidance on our pathways to expansion.

We must shift from survival mode to THRIVING. How does this happen? Through conscious evolution! And...what does that mean? *Conscious evolution is the celebratory act of leading with the soul.* It is being aware of our power to consciously choose to upgrade our lives by making choices aligned with our soul's blueprint. *It is leading with love instead of fear,* and consciously evolving beyond limitations to embrace the infinite possibilities. Let go of what no longer works in your life, and clear the way for something better suited to your ever-expanding soul.

The choice for conscious evolution is yours.
This is the path I choose for my journey. What about you?

I honor your beautiful soul and thank you for sharing the light in these messages. May they bring you a renewed sense of empowerment and joy while reminding you of the radiant being you truly are. *Amplify and share your light with the world! Enjoy the journey....it's intended to be REVOLUTIONARY!*

PART I
Expanding Perspective

1. INFINITE POSSIBILITIES

It's time for some content you can apply in your life today! *New ideas create change,* so let's look at some concepts that will trigger new thought patterns and emotional responses. All transformational information is energetic in nature. Although energy is invisible, its shifting patterns are powerful enough to transform reality.

> *Change occurs whenever anything new is created,*
> *and that change must begin within us.*

We must refocus our energy fields so our actions will correspond to these internal changes. As we accomplish this, the world around us changes in response.

We came to this life blessed with a beautiful gift: the gift of free will. To move beyond the frustration of living on auto-pilot, we must use our free will to create a more rewarding and fulfilling reality. *And it all begins with AWARENESS.* Then, we can actively identify the experiences and open the doors of possibility and experience we wish to open each day.

The possibilities are truly infinite. Our options are nearly unlimited when we do a little exploring, but *exploration cannot begin until we*

1

first become aware of ingrained behavioral patterns and subconscious default choices. Start with a little soul searching. We want to get really honest with ourselves to determine if our habits and choices are "working for us" or not.

If you are ready for expansion, **here is your first action step.**

> *Please get a notebook to write down any personal insights or "ah-ha" moments you have while reading this book. Choose an inspiring cover color and keep this notebook close by so you can record your transformation.*

First, create a "What am I Tolerating?" list.

This list is the first step in your growth and expansion. *Please write down all the habitual choices and patterns of behavior* that spring to your mind when you ask yourself that question. This list might contain anything from lack of time for yourself, to not standing up for yourself in certain situations, to not receiving the acknowledgment or love you desire. It could be surviving on a limited budget, remaining in a job you dislike, or tolerating ill health. There is no right or wrong way to do this, and your list can be as long as you wish.

Now, ask yourself: *"Which habitual choices support these intol-erable patterns in my life?"* Your answers will help identify the dis-empowering habits you must face and overcome.

This exercise, when done honestly, should be enlightening. We often don't realize how long we've tolerated unacceptable behaviors, attitudes, or habits in ourselves. We begin our expansion by establish-ing clarity regarding who and what we will tolerate in our lives. We cannot change reality until we see ourselves and our surroundings clearly.

Are you willing to create this list?

Will you say "YES!" to letting go
of everything on this list, one small step at a time?

Letting go is a process that is not accomplished all at once.
Saying "YES" will begin to clear the old limiting energy,
making you receptive to new information
and inspiration from the universe.

So, become aware of what you'd like to change, then begin building new energetic and behavioral patterns to bring about that change. Beginning with this list you will expand your awareness beyond any potentially limiting patterns and self-generated comfort zones. All possibilities exist. The lens of your consciousness determines the depth and expansiveness of your present range of possibilities.

Beyond self-imposed limitation lies an infinite field
of bright and beautiful possibilities, just waiting to be recognized.

Your life's journey is like choosing between two restaurants: One with a very uninspired, and limited number of dishes and another close by with an ever-evolving menu of tasty meals in infinite supply! Would it be more fun and exciting to have a limited, fixed menu OR would you prefer one with infinite options to select from? *I choose infinite over finite every time. Your perspective and focus will determine the expansiveness of YOUR menu.*

As children, we are often taught belief systems of finite beliefs and cultural or societal norms which reinforce lack and limitation. These childhood "stories" subconsciously mold our realities into boxes in which we are trapped. Societal, religious, or cultural "norms" can imprint false notions in the deepest recesses of our consciousness, notions that a particular gender or group has opportunities we will not have access to.

Fortunately, those "norms" and beliefs are only as true as we allow them to be. We can choose to step out of any conceptual box which makes us feel small, insignificant or incapable. We can choose to open ourselves to the possibilities available each day, to the belief that we design our own destinies. This is our birthright. ***Our beliefs can be redesigned to empower and liberate us by expanding the playing field of our life experience.*** When consciously chosen, possibilities come alive.

Infinite possibilities await our recognition daily. Infinite means ***boundless, limitless options. Not just possibilities, infinite possibilities. As we expand our beliefs, we expand our experiences.*** New doors begin to open and we discover new keys that open old doors to new possibilities. It's all about the perspective which accompanies an expansive belief in our own abilities.

You have the potential and the power to expand the number and quality of possibilities available on your journey. Open yourself to receive. By expanding your perspective, a new flood of beauty, love, abundance and prosperity will be unleashed.

> ***New opportunities wait just beyond the confines of the old, boxed-in expectations you had about yourself and your life.***

Open your heart, mind, body and spirit to this dynamic windfall of opportunities. Choose to align yourself with the brilliant light, the infinite nature of your soul. Life will begin opening up in magical new ways. You deserve this.

You have the opportunity now to break free of your old limiting beliefs and expectations, and let go of the old fears that prevent you from radiating your beautiful essence. ***Confidently declare your worth and claim the limitless options that align your life with the inherent value of your soul.*** Begin a journey that is rich, abundant and filled with possibility!

You are a part of the infinite love and intelligence of the universe, a part of the divine. Your creative potential will be awakened and nurtured by simply willing it to happen. Reality is boundless and open, so **even a slight shift in your perspective will turn a common desert into a blooming forest of infinite opportunity.** A slight adjustment to the frequency of your energy field will open a new world for you.

> ***Just as a kaleidoscope's rotation***
> ***creates a new, well-ordered pattern,***
> ***a simple rotation in your view***
> ***will bring entirely new options and opportunities.***

Alongside the visible world lies an infinite number of invisible parallel worlds, ready to emerge as your focus and perspective shifts. This knowledge is fascinating and liberating beyond description.

> You will discover new portals
> leading into new realities of your own choosing!

> ***The world beyond those gates***
> ***is where you will finally experience heaven...on earth.***

2. CHALLENGES ARE OPPORTUNITIES

Do you ever feel completely frustrated, unsettled or even scared about life? Do you feel you lack control over the direction your life is headed? Always remember your response to challenges will determine your experience.

Choose to be pro-active instead of reactive as often as possible.

Challenges can literally bring us to our knees if we allow them to, but *challenges can also open new avenues of thought, emotion, and opportunity.* Challenges clarify what we want and don't want. The contrast generates new clarity of our desires. The layers of our souls are peeled open with each challenge, giving us the chance to grow, expand, and express the beauty of our eternal spirit in new and fascinating ways. *Challenges are beautiful portals leading to discovery and personal growth.*

Some challenges, especially repeated challenges, offer deeper soul lessons. They appear with greater frequency and severity until we notice their underlying purpose. When we accept challenges as opportunities for growth and healing, they lose intensity and loosen their grip on us. With this new awareness, we can make empowered choices to shift our perception and finally overcome the most repetitive of these challenges. From our soul's perspective *challenges are simply covered jewels.*

One of our most important lessons is to flow through challenging experiences instead of fighting them every step of the way! Don't waste energy fearing a challenge because that creates a barrier against expansion. Remember that ***battling something only amplifies it*** in your experience. None of us can avoid challenges, and all of us have our own soul lessons to master.

> ***How do we master these soul lessons, so they don't repeat as the same "problem" or challenge in a new guise? By changing our responses to each challenging person or experience.***

Every challenge is a divinely designed opportunity to break a limiting cycle of thought, behavior, reaction, or communication. Don't over-analyze the situation. See it happening from a broader perspective to alleviate unnecessary struggle, tension, chaos and pain. ***We will always face challenges, but we choose the severity and the depth of the struggle as we move through the experience. The goal is to choose consciously, and not by default.*** Awareness is key.

Every moment we experience struggle or strife is another opportunity to increase the brilliance of our divine light. Struggle allows our souls to evolve. We choose the lens through which we view every relationship, person, event or experience, and ***the lens determines the result!***

Yes, life can be surprising, exciting and even daunting at times. ***It is a wild ride here on planet Earth, but it isn't meant to be a spectator sport!*** Observing life "as is" only locks it in place without the option for progression. Focus on what's possible instead of what "is." Expansion occurs deliberately, through your attention to what you wish to create and experience.

Each moment is a precious gift. Joy isn't meant to be postponed until until you reach the finish line! ***There is no finish line, the joy is always in the journey!*** Choose, beginning right now, to put yourself in the driver's seat of your spiritual vehicle and create the reality you wish to experience. Choose to refocus your energy by consciously changing the way you see, feel, and interpret your experiences. Practice feeling good! You decide whether the potholes and detours on your road to enlightenment stop you in your tracks or fuel you with greater awareness, patience and clarity.

The power to realign your world rests *WITHIN* you.

When we choose to believe our fate is in the hands of people and factors beyond our control, we forfeit our most fundamental power: the power to create our own reality! When we fail to recognize our intrinsic power, we make it that much easier for others to manipulate us and define our reality.

You have a right to create your own world in whatever way you wish. You have a divine right to expand your perspective to create different experiences. The key is acknowledging your creative power and using it to mold and design the destiny of your choice. A conscious, divinely designed destiny is not without challenges, but it generates *greater flow and harmony throughout your journey.*

Your creative power to turn challenges into opportunities for expansion involves two critical steps:

1. Change your limiting reactions, thoughts, feelings and beliefs into empowering ones
2. Learn to manage your consciousness, a process that requires consistency.

★This is a good time to reach for your paper or notebook.★

I have a practical action step for applying the insights in this chapter.

Title this action step: <u>Challenges Are Opportunities.</u>

Beginning today, actively create this new, empowering habit, retraining yourself with a new sense of awareness. Please create two columns on your piece of paper.

Title the first column: "My Habitual Reactions to Challenges."
Title the second column: "My New Empowered Responses to Challenges."

For the next few days,
focus on the way you typically react to challenges.

Write these reactions down in the first column. The next step is where the magic happens. In the second column, **choose a new, empowered response to replace the old, limiting reaction.** For example, if you typically react to a challenge by blaming someone else, you could choose "I will take accountability for my role in this." If you typically react to a challenge by yelling or going into attack mode, your new response could be "I pause, take a breath and respond in a grounded, calm way." **The goal is to become aware of old, restrictive behaviors so you can replace them with new, empowering patterns.**

As you become accountable for your response to challenges, you gain the power to overcome them. When you make new choices based on Column 2, you will stop banging your head on closed doors! I say this with love. The sooner you realize that different responses create different results, the sooner you will reap the benefits of deliberately creating your reality.

As you condition yourself to make decisions consciously
instead of impulsively, life will become more harmonious!

Set clear, positive intentions for the way you wish to approach your challenges, and the external rewards will follow suit. This higher level of awareness allows you to see challenges as opportunities. Remember, from the broader spiritual perspective, "problems" are disguised jewels offering you the gifts of strength, healing, expansion and love.

New responses reveal new solutions.

Solutions are derived from the higher energy associated with a more expansive perspective. You cannot find solutions with the same energy as your problems. They are different frequencies. As you transcend the limitations of past thinking and old patterns, you free yourself to create a new reality aligned with your new perspective.

It's important to consciously and actively unmask the false belief that you live in a world in which you are powerless. You must start with the empowered belief that you live in a world where **you have complete freedom to create your reality from the inside-out.** This empowering belief will make you thrive. Claim the power within you to create what is outside you. Release everything that no longer benefits you, so your outer world mirrors your inner self.

Your consciousness is the invisible, divine tool bestowed on you at birth, enabling you to change and shape your reality in whatever way you choose.

> ***NOW** is the time to activate your personal power to change fear into love, challenges into opportunities, and self criticism into self empowerment.*

Your creative power is limitless. Will you embrace this gift? Will you stretch and expand your awareness, and so turn your challenges into opportunities... beginning today?

3. Lifting the Veil

☨ Do you hear the inspired whispers of your soul reminding you of the truth?

☨ Can you hear your soul asking you to remember the worlds of spirit and matter are not separate?

☨ Do you ever feel that "Heaven" isn't a place far, far away or that it isn't a place at all?

"Heaven" resides within us –
within the expansiveness of our consciousness.

No airplane, spacecraft, or even bodily death is required to gain entry to this illustrious kingdom. *"Heaven" is a frequency, something we tune into, not a place we go.*

The "veil" between heaven and earth is made of light. It is spiritual energy, while all matter is simply energy in a denser form. We can create a new world within us and around us by accepting this knowledge. The divine energies within must simply be recognized before they emerge and light our pathways. The energy from these "heavenly" frequencies not only illuminates the road ahead, it points the way toward more rewarding, soulfully inspiring experiences!

Anyone can experience this. You don't have to seek a professional intuitive to gain access to the storehouse of knowledge. Are you ready, willing and open to experiencing these higher frequencies? *You can tap into your inner guidance system and be your very own "guru." You no longer need validation or approval outside yourself.*

When you access the "heavenly" frequencies, you will hold the key to an infinite source of wisdom.

So, how can you begin to connect to these spiritual frequencies? First of all, understand the distinction between intuition and higher awareness. Intuition is being in tune with ourselves. We sharpen our senses by becoming more conscious of what our bodies tell us, where our inclinations direct us, and what we "crave" in a given moment. Our intuition is developed by listening more carefully to our subtle inner voice. *We know far more than we think we do!*

To access your higher wisdom and internal GPS, and to tune in to the beings of light who exist on a higher frequency (such as angels, archangels, ascended masters, guides and loved ones who have already made their transition from the physical into the higher realms,) you must raise the vibration of your energy field.

Higher frequency is the key, but the question is: *how do you increase your energy field's vibration to reach this higher frequency?* Many frequency-raising techniques, such as meditation, are effective when used consistently. Always keep this as simple as possible.

One option: Use a mantra, a simple repeating word or phrase to saturate your entire energy field with its frequency and meaning. The goal is to quiet the mind through the power of your focus. For example, the sound "ahh" is the sound of creation. It is heard in almost every name of God: Allah, Buddha, Jehovah, God, Yahweh, and many more. *Go outside or sit in a quiet, harmonious space indoors for ten minutes each day.* Give yourself the opportunity to connect with the infinite. *Begin a new practice of conscious breathing.* Breathe in for a count of 3, then out for 3 counts. As you release your breathe, say "ahh." The power of your voice will center you and clear the pathway to higher awareness, allowing you to connect with the spiritual realms of light and love.

"Om" is another sound to use during meditation. When saying a mantra for a period of time, even for just a minute, your intuition will tell you if it resonates with you. If so, set aside at least 10 minutes in the morning, and again in the evening, to practice saying it. View this as your rejuvenation time, time you deserve for yourself! As you practice this on a consistent basis, you will begin to feel bathed in the energy of love. *Focus and visualize a golden healing light streaming into your body, from the top of your head down to your toes.* Let this light wash away any toxic thoughts, feelings, emotions and beliefs. Allow this light to increase the level of your vibration, which will amplify your intuition. *Trust this process to happen. Your belief will determine its effectiveness.*

These exercises, when applied daily, will raise your energy field to a higher frequency and transform your consciousness — all without cognitive processing! Emotional healing may simultaneously occur. If this happens, let your feelings out. Release any emotions that bubble to the surface. You may not even understand them, and you don't have to. This is a realignment, an integration of spirit and matter.

Emotional wounds and limiting beliefs slow our vibration, trapping us in a lower frequency. To gain access to the "heavenly" energies, we must connect at a high frequency. *Creating a bridge to the higher realms within our consciousness liberates the soul!*

Meditation using a mantra, and conscious breathing will align you with your true self. Consistency will yield phenomenal rewards!

Writing in a gratitude journal is another practice to integrate into your daily routine. *Listing the experiences, people, and situations for which you are thankful is a deceptively simple, but powerfully effective practice. Why? It instantly raises your vibration.* The magic of embracing gratitude shifts your focus from what is missing in your life to the beauty present at all times. As we acknowledge the blessings in our lives, we allow for even greater blessings to flow. Practicing gratitude will radically change your perspective and your emotional state, heightening the frequency of your vibrational state of being!

> *Gratitude is the quickest way to experience*
> *harmony, joy, trust, and love.*
> *It's that simple. The key is consistency.*

The application of this knowledge and the implementation of these ideas will change your life. As we lift the veil separating us from a multidimensional existence, *we embrace a new, expansive consciousness and an ever-deepening remembrance of our divine heritage. We are then open to a much broader range of energies.* These energies endow us with more creativity, authentic power, and a radiance that turns us into irresistible magnets for the joy, abundance, peace and harmony that is our birthright.

Many believe this life and this planet is all there is. Wrong! *Just because we can't see something, doesn't mean it doesn't exist.* Take love. We know it exists, we feel it! But, can we measure it or see it? No, we can't, but we know it's real. There is so much more that exists beyond the limitations of our five senses. *It is time to become multi-dimensional humans, just beyond the thresh-hold of what we previously believed was impossible.* We are on the cusp of a new humanity, a new species of spiritual beings. We must simply move beyond the old ways of seeing ourselves and the world.

Intuition and multi-sensory awareness are one in the same. Multi-sensory perception is a more expansive way of phrasing it, because the word *intuition* for many people simply means having hunches. *Multi-sensory awareness is the voice of the nonphysical world that exists within and around us at all times.*

Knowing we are more than a mind and a body will liberate us from the limitations of our five senses. We must overcome past conditioning that traps us in low frequencies, and focus on our heart- centered consciousness. That means choosing from the heart instead of from the analytical mind. *Our hearts receive and transmit higher frequency energy, so the heart remains the doorway to expansion and multi-sensory awareness.*

Now it's time for an exercise; an action step to apply this knowledge in your every day life. So,please get out your notebook.

It's application time again!

You can title this exercise:

"Expanding Beyond Five Senses to Multi-Sensory Living."

Please spend one day carefully noticing how you sense and perceive the world around you.

Below is a brief list of the five physical senses and another list with multi-sensory gifts. You will soon come to see that the five primary senses can be very limiting

FIVE SENSES

Touch, Taste, Smell, Hear and See
Visual, Auditory and Tactile Experiences

MULTI-SENSORY GIFTS and EXPANDED CONSCIOUSNESS:

Intuition
Amplified Hearing
Enhanced Touch, Taste, and Sight
Awareness of Vibrant, New Color Frequencies
Increase in Serendipity and Synchronicity
Appreciation for Stillness

Focus on Heart Centered Choices over Analytical Approaches
Telepathy
Intentional Creativity
Cellular Regeneration
Shift in the Body's Natural State of Harmony and Balance

Consciously expand your approach to life through awareness of your multi-sensory gifts. Have fun with it! This isn't meant to be drudgery. Use your notebook to document what you notice, as well as the ways you've chosen to shift beyond five sensory living. This is an exercise in remembering you are an immortal soul.

There is nothing "wrong" with enjoying your five physical senses. They are wonderful gifts. The beauty lies in broadening your human journey by using the other senses you were not previously aware of.

> *Your five basic senses are like a box of crayons containing only the basic primary colors! Choose the box with more crayons (the reality with multi-sensory perception and awareness) and you expand your options.*

You will create a far more dynamic, colorful, and beautiful life. ***Why not shift from finite to infinite or from limited to limitless? Why not bring a new, expansive "you" into being?***

To develop your multi-sensory awareness, you first need to know it exists. Next, you must tap into high energy frequencies to ***integrate this multi-sensory awareness into every-day living.***

With multidimensional perception we begin to use our:

- Clairaudience to hear messages from the spiritual realms
- Clairvoyance to see the many sights from beyond this dimension
- Clairsentience to sense/feel our way through the many versions of reality

⅄ Precognition to perceive realities we previously didn't know existed

⅄ Telekinesis to move objects with our mind

Furthermore, as our consciousness expands, we open ourselves to becoming even more telepathic. **Words aren't necessary in higher dimensional communications.** We also have the potential to become more positively empathic so we can more easily read each others thoughts and emotions.

Your personality is not your soul. Personality is your mind and body; all aspects of your physical being

> *Your soul is eternal,*
> *having existed before you were born into this lifetime,*
> *still existing after you die.*

So, lead with your soul, and experience a continual state of gratitude, vibrancy, fascination, playfulness and joy, even when life is most challenging. Multi-sensory awareness is perceiving life from a soul level, not just from the perspective of the physical body.

You have the power to lift the veil between spirit and matter, to view your life in the context of a much grander, ever-unfolding story. This includes experiences occurring simultaneously in other dimensions. Your soul is experiencing other realities and dimensions even as you read this book! You may not realize this because past conditioning keeps us focused on the physical world. Allow multi-sensory awareness to lead the way, see from a larger perspective, and let your soul lead you into greater wholeness, awareness and freedom.

> *Every experience in life is meaningful; nothing is random.*
> *Each experience and challenge has a purpose,*
> *a potential to expand your consciousness.*

Each of your experiences is perfect for the growth and expansion of your soul. Every person and situation you encounter is an opportunity for spiritual growth. Furthermore, every circumstance serves everyone involved equally. We are all beautifully assisting each other in the evolution of our uniquely designed soul journeys.

You can bridge the physical and spiritual realms now! Open up to a newly expanded awareness, realizing the veil between spirit and matter is extremely thin. ***Isn't is time to claim multi-sensory awareness and perception?*** Imagine your next experiences! Your reality will expand, and you will finally receive the love, abundance and prosperity you have always deserved.

4. SOUL SUCCESS

What is "soul success"? It's a term to describe the style of individual and group coaching and mentoring I offer my clients which *allows for "success" to be experienced in a new, expansive way.* It isn't an ego-driven style of success measured by external markers or accomplishments.

It isn't about accumulation of "things", it's about conscious creation. This is creating consistently by directing our thoughts and focus toward what we want. It is about giving our attention to only that which we wish to experience. We always receive the essence of what we think of most consistently. The key is becoming aware of the direction of our focus and realizing that we are never rewarded for struggle. We are rewarded by remembering that whatever we give our attention to is a direct invitation for its manifestation.

Soul success stems from the yearnings and desires of your limitless, eternal self. *It is rooted within you, free from external constraints or superficial requirements.* You feel alive when liberated from the distractions and limitations of the external world. You feel empowered when you remember that *you are a walking, talking, vibrational magnet* that attracts whatever you shine the spotlight of your focus upon!

> *This is inside-out instead of outside-in success at its finest!*
> *(the only kind of success worthy of sustaining.)*

Are you ready to awaken and energize your spirit, to be reminded of your true power and potential? Well, that is precisely what I wish for you. It's time to tap into the infinite well of divine consciousness to create new pathways for creative expression, growth, and fulfillment.

"Soul Success" keeps you in tune with the frequencies of abundance, prosperity and JOY. It's your birthright, so claim it!

And remember, there is no excitement or power in creating your life on auto-pilot! As you become consciously pro-active instead of reactive and find reasons each day to celebrate yourself, your life and those around you, your life will transform.

To experience soul-driven success, it might be necessary to identify your current definition of success and expand upon it to allow for even greater results.

With that said, it's application time again!

Please title this exercise:

"WHAT DOES SOUL SUCCESS MEAN TO ME?"

This exercise will help you clarify what's important to you, as well as make you aware of earlier definitions of "success" which may be holding you back.

To *tap into your limitless, dynamic creative potential,* please answer the following questions:

What was my definition of success growing up?

Is this definition accurate, and is it still applicable to me?

What kind of soul-driven success do I want to achieve NOW?

Do my present thoughts, feelings and actions allow me to generate the results I deserve?

Please list the physical, mental, emotional, spiritual and financial rewards you want to achieve with a new, expanded version of "soul success." Gain clarity on the WHY'S and let go of figuring out the HOW'S.

Next to the "rewards," **list the affirmative thoughts, feelings and actions** which will align your consciousness with these rewards.

Review this exercise often. Remember your power to manifest new opportunities every day. Choose to generate expansive success in your life.

Your emotional, mental and action patterns determine what you attract into your life, so they are essential ingredients in the creation of the abundance, harmony and fulfillment you wish to experience.

The average human has around 50,000 thoughts every day, but 99% are exactly the same ones we had yesterday! Thought patterns, once ingrained, form subconscious attitudes. So the greatest danger is forming negative attitudes because they limit our expectations. Subconscious cycles of negative thinking leave us unaware of our potential, when we should be pro-actively creating our lives.

We must consciously open our minds to the limitless possibilities available to us. **Anyone who believes they are stuck in their current circumstances due to their upbringing, education, parents or past experiences is unnecessarily limiting themselves.** Choose to tap into the power of the creative force of your mind. Realize your freedom to choose your thoughts, attitudes, beliefs, and actions, paving the way for authentic, lasting "soul success."

You are the only one capable of creating the life you dream of. No one can do it for you. You must choose to be a soulfully "rich" or "wealthy" individual. Authentic "soul success" yields rewards which are felt from within and naturally permeate every area of our lives. Wealth is not measured by the accumulation of external objects. It is inside-out wealth, not outside-in.

Experiencing "soul success" is an inside job. Nothing in the material world has the power to make us feel soulfully successful. No amount of money, power, or prestige will ever be enough to satisfy that inner thirst for spiritual fulfillment. This may be why you are reading this book right now.

I encourage you to trust yourself by creating the success YOUR soul craves. There is no "right" or "wrong" way to do this. There is simply harmony or disharmony resulting from your choices.

Just remember to ask yourself the following questions:

"What kind of success do I truly crave?"

"What experiences do I wish to have?"

"WHY do I wish to experience this?
What feelings will it generate?"

"Am I currently expecting and experiencing this success?"

If not, all it takes is awareness. Shift your intentions to positively support the new, more authentic model of success which is perfectly aligned with your spirit.

Begin to feel the essence of what you wish to experience NOW instead of waiting for the end result.

Why not say "yes?" You have everything to gain and nothing to lose. Your soul will celebrate your expanded expectations of "success", and you will attract the experiences, and people to support a higher level of fulfillment. Open your heart. Raise the vibration of your energy field to expand your reality. This self-selected reality with ***soulfully inspired success is waiting to be claimed...***

5. ACCOUNTABILITY

Accountability: a word that should be very empowering! Unfortunately, it often feels heavy and generates negative emotion. My intention is to use the word to inspire positive change. The word accountability has two components, 'account' and 'ability', which we will use to **create a much broader definition!**

Our new definition of accountability:

> *An individual drive, desire, and willingness to account for the life we are experiencing from moment to moment rooted in pure empowerment of the soul.*

As we enter into this conversation about accountability, it's important to do so with a large dose of **self-love and self-compassion**. It takes tremendous courage to address our inner roadblocks, yet this is precisely what offers us the opportunity for greater success, love, connection and harmony in our day-to-day lives!

I wish to remind you that you are perfectly lovable just as you are! You are worthy of love, abundance and success just as you are now. Your past programming or old patterns or limiting beliefs can be released beginning now. **How you feel about yourself NOW is your responsibility.** THAT you can change and heal. When you step into personal accountability for our own feelings and beliefs, the old negative patterns and energy unwind and release – freeing you to experience life in brand new ways.

Stepping into harmony with yourself and generating profound inner peace and contentment from within is not a result of "fixing yourself."

You are not broken — you are a beautiful, precious soul.
It is a tremendous relief to discover you are not flawed.

The intention with this information is to empower you to simply step beyond any self-created limitations and allow your innate brilliance and beauty to shine through. When you discover this truth for yourself, old patterns of dis-empowered living will fall away, leaving only the purity and perfection of you as a soul. Then, the options are limitless!

When you own your experiences and choose to accept full responsibility for all you create, repel, or attract into your experience, *you will hold the key to proactive success*! After an honest self-evaluation, you may not like everything about your current circumstances, but recognize your ability to change. *The circumstances you've attracted are the results of the energy vibrations you've sent out (consciously or unconsciously.)* This may be a challenging to accept, but it is the key to your liberation and freedom.

When you choose better feeling thoughts, take deliberate positive action and assume responsibility for all you create, you will reap the benefits of "accountability."

Being the only one to steer your spiritual vehicle is very empowering.
No one else has power over your life unless
you hand over the steering wheel.

Claim your creative birthright b*y assuming control over your day to day encounters and experiences. Blame and excuses are traits of people who have forfeited their creative power.* If you notice yourself consistently finding others at fault for your unsatisfactory experiences, or you make excuses for your inability to positively affect a situation or outcome, you limit your ability to create a fulfilling life! Lead with self-love and self-compassion and awaken your creative abilities by stepping into the role of conscious creator. This is an opportunity you can seize at anytime, and now is a perfect time to start.

The greatest gift you can offer yourself and your loved ones is to say to them:

"MY HAPPINESS DEPENDS ON ME – SO YOU'RE OFF THE HOOK! I am responsible for how I feel and I will no longer rely on you to determine my mood or state of well-being. I claim my power and will no longer use you as an excuse to be unhappy."

It is only when we take personal accountability for what we are feeling that our wounds are unveiled and become consciously accessible to us. When we distract ourselves and focus outwardly on another person, we throw a layer of denial over our wounds, giving up our access to them. What we want most in the moment we are emotionally triggered is to acknowledge and open the underlying wound. *There is a part of us that is desperate for our own attention, acceptance and love.* We don't have to analyze, defend, justify or figure out the source of our wounds. We simply have to acknowledge them, and then claim our power to make new empowered choices. These new choices will allow for greater love, harmony and happiness!

> *If we become aware of and STOP the blame game –*
> *the habit to fix, judge, blame or attack someone else –*
> *and consciously take accountability for what we are*
> *experiencing, we bring our energy and attention*
> *back to ourselves, where we most need it.*

The truth is that all relationships are mirrors. They are gifts offering us the opportunity to see how much love we are offering ourselves – or not! As we practice personal accountability for our own feelings and healing, we come to REALIZE that *we love others exactly the way we love ourselves!*

So, if you are judging, blaming and attacking someone else, it is only because at the deepest level you are judging, blaming and attacking yourself. If you are struggling to love someone, you are having a hard time loving the part of yourself that is being reflected to you from that individual. All relationships mirror the way we feel about and treat ourselves. *The purpose of relationships is to show us where we need to heal and bring love to ourselves.* Essentially, we live in a world of mirrors! In our humanness, we are all "works in progress." We need to practice forgiving ourselves as well as each other, which ends up being the same thing!

> *Recognizing limiting, self-sabotaging patterns rooted in "not my fault" living is the first step toward accountable living.*

Your willingness to take responsibility for your choices and actions is vital in breaking free of old limits. You relinquish your power when you blame external forces for your circumstances. You liberate yourself when you own your experiences. Take ownership of your life! You will feel empowered beyond measure.

Take responsibility to direct your own experience from the inside-out. It is your path to freedom, to create the life of your dreams. Make clear conscious choices, knowing you are solely responsible for your responses to challenges. Even when you cannot directly control events, you can determine how you will respond.

> *Situations can be disasters or*
> *opportunities to learn and grow.*
> *It's all a matter of perspective.*

Each event is the result of the choices you've made, and all these events are divinely designed to help your soul expand.

Actively listen to yourself and observe how you think, speak, and react to coworkers, family members, and friends. You may just realize you have been giving your power away by being unaccountable. That can all change beginning now!

Claim your power and spread your wings! Once you experience accountable living, your soul will soar on its own.

Accountable living involves four stages.

1. **"I Am Not Responsible"** - *for anything that has happened/ is happening to me.*

    At first we believe life is happening to us rather than through us. We choose to believe we have neither control nor options. This stage is rooted in the core belief of victimization.

2. **"I Intend to Accept Responsibility"** - *in this particular moment.*

    Second, we choose to review past experiences and events during which we made no conscious choices. We must honestly face the feelings of guilt, shame or resentment, because *we* cannot change what we refuse to recognize.

3. **"I AM Responsible"** - *in the moment.*

    Then comes the true potential for expansion. A spark of ownership flares to life along with a conscious willingness to change. We begin to feel the power to influence our current circumstances. We feel a renewed sense of authority, and become eager to design our destinies by choosing our own experiences.

4. **"I AM Responsible For Everything"**

Finally, we feel an unwavering dedication to transforming every experience to reflect our souls' truest desires. There is a highly conscious, proactive involvement at all levels of being (mental, physical, emotional and spiritual), a fully empowered decision to guide our own expansion.

It's application time again!

Please take out your notebook and title this exercise:

GROWING FROM BLAME INTO ACCOUNTABILITY.

First, a few tips:

- ⚔ *Listen to the voice in your head. Is it positive or negative?* Commit today: Eliminate blame. Eliminate excuses. Take active responsibility for your decisions and your life.

- ⚔ *Listen to yourself speak.* Do you blame others for things that don't go exactly as you want? Do you point fingers at your partner, your coworkers, or your parents? *Are you making excuses for unmet goals*? You can change all these patterns of blame right now.

- ⚔ If someone you respect tells you that you are making excuses or blaming others for your woes, take the feedback seriously. Look within; do some soul searching.

- ⚔ Consciously *change old defensive patterns and craft positive new responses.* Deepen your understanding of partners, coworkers, and friends, and do this with a renewed sense of compassion.

- ⚔ *The next time you catch yourself making an excuse, whether it's for a late project, an unmet goal, an unfulfilled career, or an*

unfulfilled life, gently remind yourself – "NO EXCUSES."
Instead, spend your time focusing on your next soulfully
successful venture. Choose to make <u>positive thinking</u> a new
empowering habit, and remember that excuses only fuel
a sense of inner failure. Your soul deserves more and so
do YOU.

Excuses for failure, bad choices, and limited accomplishments only
fuel a sense of dis-empowerment – and lead to undesirable actions
and behaviors. Excuses block you from success and joy. *Isn't it time
to step out of that box?*

Take an honest inventory of your behavior.

**Read through the following questions and make a list of
those that ring true.**

Label the first column: *Lingering Excuses*

Label the second column: **New Empowered Decisions**

Now, it's time to get real with yourself. When you listen to the
words running through your mind and the words coming out of
your mouth, which excuses do you hear most often? Which new
empowered choice could replace that excuse? Keep adding to your
list until you've uncovered every hidden saboteur in your consciousness. *It's time to let self-empowerment and self love guide your choices.*

Once you've completed this exercise, applaud yourself for being
courageous enough to address the inner roadblocks. You are giving
yourself the opportunity for greater success, love, connection and
harmony.

*Stepping into harmony with yourself and generating profound inner
peace and contentment isn't a result of "fixing yourself."* Spiritual

expansion is the result of making lasting changes at to the core of your being. It is the result of remembering who you are and discovering you are already whole. It is the realization of your infinite, divine nature.

> *It is a tremendous relief to discover you are not flawed.*
> *You must simply step beyond the self-created limitations*
> *to allow your innate brilliance and beauty to shine through.*

When you discover this truth for yourself, old patterns of dis-empowered living will fall away, leaving only the purity and perfection of you as a soul. The options are limitless.

6. Transcending Limits

Your personal beliefs play a powerful role in determining your quality of life because they frame your view of everything around you! Your experiences create your perceptions of reality, so *your belief system must be fluid enough to allow for the growth brought about by those experiences.*

> *Rigidly held views will only limit your experience.*
> *A belief is simply a thought you keep thinking.*
> *Therefore, they change as YOU change.*

Limiting behaviors follow limiting beliefs because those beliefs will determine how you interpret life. Restrictive beliefs narrow your perspective and make you feel less empowered. *Powerlessness is a clear indicator that you are out of alignment with who you really are.*

What is a Limiting Belief?

A belief is a conviction or generalization you accept as truth without positive proof or knowledge. A *limiting* belief is one that prevents you from achieving your full potential.

A Limiting Belief...

- fools you into not trying.
- blinds you to the expansive options available.
- restricts your choices.
- stops you from taking risks.
- keeps you stuck.

- obstructs your growth.
- keeps you repeating negative patterns.
- prevents you from taking responsibility for your life.
- prevents you from pursuing your dreams.
- promotes a victim mentality.
- encourages procrastination.
- gives you endless excuses for not following your dreams.
- fills you with guilt, doubt, and fear.
- helps you find "evidence" to support limits
- stops you from imagining the possibilities.
- makes you feel negative and discontented.
- halts breakthroughs.

Beliefs are not facts, but are often more powerful because they are the prism through which we see reality.

Common Limiting Beliefs

Listen carefully to yourself. Do you restrict yourself with limits like:

- I don't deserve success.
- I never have enough time or money.
- I don't have any support.
- It's just not possible.
- I'm not good at this.
- Others can do it better.
- I'm not experienced enough.
- I'm not beautiful enough.
- I'm not smart enough.
- I'm not important enough.
- I'm too young.
- I'm too old.
- I don't have the energy.
- I always get sick this time of year.
- It's just not in my genes.

⅄ It's too hard.

⅄ It never works for me.

⅄ I'm too lazy.

⅄ That happens to other people.

⅄ Nobody ever notices me.

⅄ I never get what I want.

⅄ This is just "the way it is."

⅄ I have no control over this.

⅄ I have nothing to offer

⅄ I'm always overlooked.

⅄ This always happens to me.

⅄ I never win anything.

⅄ I have terrible luck.

By simply being aware, you can break out of these self-made boxes! **Belief systems either empower or restrict.** Which beliefs support you? Which keep you stuck? Beliefs are built on varying degrees of optimism AND pessimism, and they determine what you think you are capable of experiencing.

> *You can mold your beliefs to reflect the*
> *successful life you wish to experience.*

You weren't born with belief systems in place! You either created them or accepted what you were taught! Just as you created them, you can RE-create them if they are restricting you. Many belief systems were developed and accepted without question during childhood, but you can break through any dis-empowering mental barriers, move beyond self-constructed limitations, and live in a world of unlimited possibilities.

It all begins with your thoughts, which reinforce your potential or harden your limitations. Everything you were ever taught about the world around you became a building block for your current belief systems. But now you have the ability to CHOOSE which thoughts and ideas to accept.

> *Discipline your focus!*
> *If you allow fear-based thoughts, you will create a fearful world.*
>
> *But if you focus on your strengths, abilities,*
> *and the limitless opportunities available to you –*
> *you will attract experiences aligned with these expansive beliefs.*
>
> *Look around you. Your external world always reflects your beliefs.*
> *It mirrors your inner world.*

Your reality is based on the consistently held thoughts, words, actions and beliefs which make up your consciousness. So, take an honest look at your life, including your environment, relationships, finances, and health. What you see around you is a reflection of your internal reality.

Those who remain "poor" do so because they live with a poverty belief system. Their thoughts and acts reflect an impoverished mentality springing from a poverty belief system. No one consciously chooses to be poor, but unless we build a belief system, thought by thought and action by action, that reflects an optimistic perspective on life, we will remain "poor." This is the reason so many lottery winners end up broke! Their core beliefs and low energy frequency do not support over-flowing, permanently held abundance.

It's been said that if you took all the money in the world and divided it up equally among all the people, it would eventually end up right back where it started. Why? *A poverty mindset will attract poverty and a wealthy mindset will attract wealth. So, which do you choose?* Yes, this is a choice! This isn't out of your control. No matter how you grew up or what your past was like, you can develop a new mindset RIGHT NOW with awareness, determination, and deliberate focus. *You cannot receive abundance without a mindset rooted in abundance.*

Aside from your thoughts, pay close attention to your words. *What you say is a critical indicator of your belief systems.* Have you ever noticed what people living in poverty or ill health talk about? They talk about lack, time and time again. So, take note of the words coming out of your mouth! If you find yourself saying anything that begins with "I can't," or "Nothing ever," immediately replace them with statements beginning with "I am" or "I will," or "Everything does.." The key is noticing how often your words and thoughts sabotage your own life experience. Become aware of what you're doing, and you will have the power to create positive change in your life!

Negative thoughts are the building blocks for negative experiences, while positive thoughts lead to positive experiences.

It's that simple! Worrying about something doesn't change it. In fact, it only attracts more worry because that is where you focus your attention. Where you choose to focus today will determine the people, circumstances and opportunities (or lack of opportunities) you will attract into your experience tomorrow.

To understand your limiting beliefs on a deeper level, address their roots. *Oftentimes, beliefs are imprints of experiences from other lifetimes. Examples of "core" imprints are abandonment, unworthiness, betrayal, inadequacy, and rejection.* Any negative core imprints will accompany you from lifetime to lifetime until you notice them, accept responsibility for their creation, and neutralize them. Your history as a soul is recorded in the "akashic records," which are are located in the etheric plane. These files are an archive of holographic data containing the soul records of all humanity. Your personal file contains your information from every dimension, star system, galaxy and universe. It contains your core imprints. You can ask your spiritual support team in the non-physical realms for access to these records during your meditations. Ask for revelations about your core imprints and, if necessary, ask for help in creating a more positive belief system. Ask to be released from any soul contracts that no longer help you grow. Be patient with this process.

It's application time!

Please take out your notebooks and title this exercise:

Transcending Limiting Beliefs.

Please create two columns on two separate pages.

Title the first column: **My Core Beliefs.**
Title the second column: **I AM Intentions.**

The intentions will be used to neutralize any limiting core beliefs about life, love, and your potential. *In the first column, write down all your limiting core beliefs.* Negative core beliefs are strongly-held, rigid, and inflexible. They are maintained by the tendency to focus on information that supports the belief while ignoring evidence that contradicts it. They become the very essence of how you see yourself, others, the world, and the future.

Examples of limiting core beliefs are:

"I am unlovable."
"People always reject me."
"The world is a dangerous place."
"The future is hopeless."
"There must be something wrong with me."
"I am powerless to change my life."
"I am inferior to others."

Ask yourself if these beliefs have to do with abandonment, unworthiness, betrayal, inadequacy, or rejection.

> *Look at your life and notice how these core beliefs*
> *are consistently revealed in your experiences and relationships.*

Challenging Your Negative Core Beliefs

*To evaluate and challenge your core beliefs, ask yourself
"Which experiences show this belief is not
completely true all the time?"*

List as many experiences as you can, and be as specific as possible. Write down everything even if you're not sure they are relevant. When you have considered all the experiences, develop an alternative, more balanced core belief. Remember these experiences prove your negative core belief is not completely true all the time. Can you think of any more appropriately balanced and helpful core beliefs?

Write these down.

On the next page, create a second column.

Write an intention beginning with the words "I am."

Intentions fuel positive thinking, so use these intentions to neutralize your negative core beliefs. Here are some examples of the "I AM Intentions" you can use in this exercise.

"I am capable beyond measure."
"I am in charge of creating my destiny."
"I am whole and complete."
"I am surrounded by love."
"I am an integral part of the divine plan."
"I am bathed in the light of acceptance."
"I am aware of my true value and worth."
"I am divinely guided and protected."
"I am at peace with myself and with life."
"I am trusting of myself and others."
"I am a powerful, eternal being with limitless potential."

Set the intention to over-write the negative imprints and associated limiting core beliefs. Neutralize the negative imprints with the power of your "I am" intention statements. Affirm the following: ***"All negative core imprints in my belief system are now being neutralized. All my thoughts are shifting into perfect balance. I am liberated and free!"***

Begin to consciously, deliberately, and purposefully create the belief systems that will empower you. Your belief systems will always be validated in your experiences. You will always find evidence to support your beliefs and confirm them to be true for you. If your current 'truths' aren't ones you want to support or perpetuate, change them.

Remember, a belief is just a thought you keep thinking! No one else can choose your thoughts for you! The ball is in YOUR COURT at all times. YOU determine the quality of your life experience. Why not make it a phenomenal one?

7. Transcending Attachments

Spiritual Surrender is the process of releasing attachments, a key component of harmonious living. ***Attachments to people, objects, labels, expectations, outcomes, beliefs, and perspectives can be unhealthy if motivated by fear of loss.***

Want a clear indicator of attachment? Anytime you are in reaction mode, you are attached to something. You are looking through a small lens at how things "should" be, and reacting when all doesn't go according to your plan. This causes tension as well as anxiety, frustration, and even anger. A stressful or tight sensation in the body is a clear signal that you are trying to control your life or control certain outcomes.

The symptoms of unhealthy attachments are fear and anxiety, caused by the need to control. ***The need to control stems from fear of loss.*** Unfortunately, the desire for continuity and security cannot be satisfied externally. True security and protection are generated and sustained from within. They can't be validated outside ourselves.

> ***We must free our spirits and lighten our grips***
> ***because fear is a magnet for experiences***
> ***which validate our belief in an unsafe world.***

We must embrace more positive, empowering beliefs about the world, and our connection to it. Let go of the limiting beliefs which cause struggle and turmoil, and replace them with beliefs which attract abundance, joy and love into your life!

Attachments to a particular identity, status, label, outcome or expectation keep you unconsciously trapped in a very small box. There is no freedom inside a box! As long as we need things to happen a certain way, or feel dependent upon external validation, we are allowing the ego's demand for control to take us out of the flow.

Demands on others or on life diminish and deplete our energy.
By letting go, we are liberated.

In seeking security and happiness through control or through the accumulation of material objects, soul-fulfillment eludes us. Happiness comes from within. Any joy derived from external attachments will be fleeting; ego-excitement will subside, and we will still be searching for something to fill the void. This search becomes an endless cycle until we realize true contentment flows from self acceptance and unconditional love of ourselves.

The source of happiness resides within us, not outside us.
Accepting this is one of our greatest challenges in life,
but once mastered, the rewards are priceless.

Actively striving for detachment (this does not equate to not caring) puts us on a direct path to authentic success and happiness. *When our sense of self is detached from status, finance, or emotional desperation and need, the stage is set for authentic soul success.* There is nothing wrong with having a beautiful home, nice things, or relationships grounded in deep connection. However, if we need that home or object or person to sustain our worthiness, security, or status, they will become our prison guards. Neediness leads to attachment, to a dependency on relationships or external validation which is self-defeating. Life becomes unstable, an emotional rollercoaster. Attachment = conditional love. Our souls crave balance, unconditional love, and acceptance of others and ourselves. It is up to us to embrace it.

By loving unconditionally, we allow our loved ones the freedom to be themselves in the most authentic way possible. We have no desire to control, manipulate, or direct their behavior. ***If we require someone to behave in a particular we are not offering love, but unhealthy attachment.*** This prison can only be escaped through genuine love and acceptance. Love and forgiveness dissolve cords of attachment. Shame and guilt bind us to past memories which limit our future. True liberation comes when we release all the cords which bind us to anything outside ourselves.

> ***When we accept others without trying to change or mold them, they naturally reveal their best to us.***

This process begins with self acceptance. We accept ourselves, and naturally accept those around us. When the people in our lives feel freely accepted as they are, their best qualities shine through. All the qualities we could ever want in a family or partner are revealed effortlessly when we refrain from judging. With acceptance and love, magic happens!

It's application time again!

Please take out your notebook and title this exercise:

Exploring My Attachments.

As you honestly explore your attachments, you will re-discover your personal freedom. Step into the flow, where the magic happens!

Awareness is the key to change and expansion. Review the information below and *notice what rings true for you.* Please be honest with yourself.

> ***Make a list of your attachments to people, ideas, beliefs, labels, objects or perspectives which cause anxiety and stress.***

⚔ **Attachments to people prevent us from examining ourselves**. Do you have a tendency to cling to your partner, friends or loved ones, fearing they may leave you? Clinging to someone in a relationship masks an underlying lack of self-worth. You will benefit greatly from your own loving exploration of yourself. Take the focus off others to see which thoughts, feelings, insecurities and dreams are dwelling inside you. Trust yourself to explore your own fear and passions.

⚔ **Attachments to identities/labels keep us imprisoned**. Are there any labels you require from others to feel successful or loved? Must you look and dress a certain way, or drive a certain car to feel accepted by society? Is there an external identity you are afraid to lose? Are these identities empowering you or locking you in a small box?

⚔ **Attachments reveal a fear of not being in control**. If you were hurt, abandoned, abused or criticized in your past, it's understandable you fear "letting go" to trust completely. But, would you be willing to do something differently to allow for greater harmony in your relationships, business or health? Will you loosen your grip and befriend an unknown which holds beautiful new opportunities for love and success beyond your wildest imagination? Will you step into the flow and accept life as it happens?

⚔ **Controlling what others say or do causes separation instead of connection.** Do you "know" how your partner, children, boss, parents, and co-workers "should" be? Turn the coin over and see how you feel when others "know" how YOU should be! Rather than resisting and creating conflict, stay grounded and accepting. Reactive behavior is rooted in fear and confusion. Allow others to be themselves, stop judging them, and you will open new doors of opportunity and connection instead of building walls of separation. The rewards are priceless.

⊥ **Attachments to possessions or money are rooted in fear**. Do your possessions define you? What if they were taken away? Would you feel empty? Lost? Begin to embrace the true qualities within yourself and others. Cherish your relationships, and acknowledge the joy and love they contribute to your life. Stop focusing on the fleeting "high" you get from purchasing something! Remember, when your life is over, you don't take anything with you except the love in your heart and the lessons you learned along the way.

⊥ **Focusing on what you don't have is a waste of energy.** Focusing on what you don't have keeps you trapped in a cycle of lack. When you chase people, money or material objects, you have no time to appreciate the blessings which already exist! The key to greater love, abundance, joy, and success is focusing on the beauty and gifts you have NOW. Wanting generates more wanting, but gratitude opens door to greater blessings.

⊥ **Attachments to old, limiting belief systems is like living in a small box**. Everywhere you turn, you bump into another wall. Let go of a belief if it no longer contributes to your health, wealth, and happiness! Expand beyond the limiting beliefs of your past. *Let go of anything that keeps you living in a "consciousness shack" instead of a "consciousness mansion."*

⊥ **When attachments fall away, only the truth remains.** Shed limiting attachments, and life becomes magical, miraculous and beautiful beyond measure.

Letting go is essential for lasting harmony and inner peace. Releasing attachments is a moment-to-moment choice, a natural by-product of leading with your soul. Stop depending on anything or anyone outside you for happiness or feelings of "success". Stop trying to control the world around you. Then, *the Universe will surprise and delight you in beautiful new ways.*

8. INNER WORTH AND OUTER WEALTH

Just imagine … any amount of wealth can be yours! Picture your life enriched by the most fulfilling relationships imaginable! Think of spending your time doing only those things you love and, in return, experiencing abundance that once seemed impossible!

The processes of generating inner worth and outer wealth are inextricably linked!

> *The more worthiness you feel internally,*
> *the greater wealth you attract externally.*

Wealth of "being" occurs when the essence of our spiritual selves is infused throughOUT our lives. It is fulfillment growing from the inside-out, rooted in a peace of mind independent of external reinforcement. Living in alignment with our authentic selves, we experience wealth from the inside out – with the richness of our inner world reflected in our outer lives. We thrive on a sense of wholeness, harmony, fluidity and grace.

Self-esteem inspires wealth consciousness!

> *The value we see in ourselves creates the*
> *abundance we are open to receiving.*

Self-worth opens us to receive love, money, opportunity and success without limits, so our inner worth must be recognized and cultivated before we achieve external success. The ability to attract friends, clients, and financial opportunities, as well as to live abundant, wealthy lifestyles (inside and out) stems from a self-generated and self-perpetuated expansive mind set. This frame of mind expects wealth because it is rooted in the sincere belief that we are worthy of all forms of riches.

There are a myriad of ways to **nurture self-esteem**. Try these out for yourself!

1. **Rise above the expectations of others.** Stop berating yourself for not living up to someone else's ideals. Conforming to obtain the approval of others is a sure-fire path to low self-esteem. Identify what's important to YOU and strive to be YOUR best, leaving the opinions and judgments of others behind. This brings immediate relief.

2. **Release perfectionism.** No one is perfect! Striving for perfection is a futile waste of energy. Relax more. Trust you are growing and evolving at the speed best suited to YOU.

3. **Make a list of your positive attributes**, including skills, experiences, physical and social resources, talents, or anything else that makes you feel good about yourself. Add to the list any compliments others have given you. Reminding yourself of all your qualities is a sure confidence booster. Then, read it often!

4. **Stop settling. No more Excuses!** Your life experiences offer the opportunity to refine your preferences (in your partner, habits, health, career) Integrate life's lessons by being more selective in who and what you allow in your life!

5. **Celebrate your personal wins on a daily basis!** Your accomplishments are valuable. Focus your attention on what's working in your life!

It is your birthright to be spiritual AND wealthy! Any belief to the contrary is a roadblock preventing you from experiencing the success you deserve.

Limiting beliefs become deeply ingrained at an early age, and remain roadblocks to success because they are rooted in a worldview of scarcity. ***Become aware of self-imposed limits.*** This is the first step in transforming old constraints into empowering motivations that allow you to experience the wealth and happiness you desire.

> ***ATTRACT THE SUCCESS you so richly***
> ***deserve by first believing you are worthy.***

Our thoughts, beliefs and expectations determine whether money is drawn to us or repelled by us. If you believe it's too hard to make money, that belief will become reality.

> ***Your experiences always validate your beliefs. It's that simple.***

You will make generating money too great a challenge if that's what you expect! If you believe it's not possible to be rich, you won't be! Replace those limiting beliefs with a recognition of your inherent worthiness. ***Your thoughts and beliefs must align with your goal of creating and attracting wealth.***

Your current financial situation is a direct result of your beliefs about the (non) scarcity of money, your worthiness to receive it, and your ability to manage it. ***To create a better financial situation, you must think differently.*** You must believe you deserve it! You must identify and confront any thoughts, attitudes, feelings, or behaviors that keep you trapped in a limited lifestyle. ***You must to be willing to make changes.*** Change can be scary, but it's the key to liberation, success and financial freedom! Inspired change empowers you from the inside-out.

Create a new vision for your life – right now. Believe in your inner worth and develop a wealthy mind-set. Make change happen now by an unblinking examination of your current beliefs. Are they limiting your ability to attract wealth? *Clearly examine your relationships, lifestyle, business, and health. See yourself flourishing. See yourself succeeding.* Visualize the best possible scenario for yourself and your family. Don't hold back. What would your ideal life look like? *Visualize your boldest dream.* Believe in yourself.

Today is the first day of a new abundant, prosperous life! You are an infinitely creative being, so take the first step. *Create a new, liberating habit of launching into each day with a sense of positive expectation coupled with empowered imagination. You will achieve phenomenal success,* and it all begins inside.

Remember, you deserve wealth.

You deserve success.

Step up and seize it!

Inner worth is the catalyst for limitless abundance and happiness. Make a fresh start by incorporating only positive new beliefs into your mindset. Forgive yourself and others. *Release any criticism of yourself or intolerance of others to clear away the roadblocks to your success!*

Commit to nurturing your self-confidence, and you will find that nothing is out of reach. This is how you begin to achieve the most rewarding levels of wealth, expansion, and inner peace.

Always remember that experiencing heightened levels of vitality, optimal health, inner worth and outer wealth truly IS an inside job!

IT'S APPLICATION TIME AGAIN!

Please take out your notebooks and title this exercise:

MY DAILY ENERGY TUNE-UP!

> *Establishing inner worth and outer wealth IS an inside job, therefore you must acknowledge the role your energy field plays in the creation of your experiences.*

Your energy field needs regular tune-ups just like your car. In fact, your energy field benefits from a daily tune up, not just an occasional one. This will increase self-worth, amplify your confidence and pave the way for a wealthy, abundant lifestyle.

Begin by evaluating all the aspects of your consciousness that affect your energy field, including your most repetitive thoughts, emotions, statements, and actions. Make certain you are positive and expansive in all you do or think.

Positive self nurturing habits and routines will bolster your spirit and remind you of your power to create a wonder-full, successful life, keeping you on a high, clear and magnetic frequency.

Create *empowering new rituals* for yourself beginning right NOW!

Tune in daily to ask the following questions as part of your **ENERGY TUNE UP**:

⅄ *Are my thoughts and emotions aligned with my spirit's desire for joy, success and abundance?*

⅄ *Do my words reflect my spirit's intentions and desires for inner worth and outer wealth?*

⅄ ***Do my actions support the expression of my soul's desire for health, harmony and happiness?***

With an honest look at the life you're currently creating, you have the opportunity to allow for new, expansive results! These results will align with your dreams and desires, as well as nourish your soul. This is your divine birthright. ***Now, ALLOW bliss, health and wealth into your daily experience.***

The expansive nature of your consciousness determines the quality of your experiences. Activate your personal power by giving your energy field a daily tune-up, placing yourself in the driver's seat for your journey. Now, steer your spiritual and physical vehicle with conscious awareness, clarity and purpose. Begin today. You have nothing to lose and everything to gain!

9. Seize the Moment

Every moment offers opportunities to share love, be loved, extend forgiveness, and heal our hearts. Are you willing to seize THIS moment, to experience greater peace, harmony and connection in your life? *You cannot "seize the day" without embracing and enjoying the moments that make up the day!*

> *The joy is in the journey, not just the destination.*
> *There is NO power in "then" or "later"!*
> *Bliss happens NOW.*

So, "Claim it NOW!" Embrace the beauty. FEEL. BE. KNOW. EXPERIENCE. Don't wait. Life is precious, and fleeting.

We spend so much time time worrying about the future or the past. The present moment is all that exists, so don't let the past or future intrude. *Ignore the past, leave the future to itself, and simply be "present" in the moment. This is where your creative power resides.* Attempts to relive the past or control the future cause immeasurable stress and heartache because they are rooted in fear. Priceless moments, meant to be savored, are here right now! LIVE NOW!

Stop looking for external validation for your accomplishments. Seek your own validation as you relax into the flow of each moment. This doesn't mean you withdraw into a lotus position and meditate alone all day. Far from it! It means you enjoy the moments of your life by embracing opportunities as they arise. It means choosing actions, behaviors, and interactions that are positive, beneficial, and meaningful to your personal and spiritual growth.

> *Don't analyze the past and future so much you*
> *take all the fun out of the present!*

No need to wait for tomorrow to feel love, notice beauty, or experience joy! You don't have to wait to be happy. Don't postpone your joy by waiting for some future event like retirement, a vacation, or a promotion to experience happiness! Don't postpone your bliss for some later moment! You will miss opportunities today if you are worrying about the future or dwelling in the past. One no longer exists, and the other isn't here yet. There is no better time than the present.

So, FORGET Carpe Diem! Instead, embrace CARPE MOMENTO. Seizing the moment is a gift you give yourself right NOW. Your only guarantee in life is that you have each MOMENT to live, respond, act, and feel however you choose. So, does it make sense to worry about the future or the past?

> *Worrying is praying for an outcome you don't want. Focus your*
> *energy on what you want to create instead of what you fear.*

Have you heard the voice inside you crying out to feel alive, vital and passionate in the moment? Not tomorrow, not next year. Your soul yearns for vitality... NOW! Passion fueled by the soul should be experienced each moment. *Joy is self-generated. It doesn't fall into your lap after something external happens.* It exists each precious moment, just waiting for you to acknowledge it.

Why not begin today? Make a conscious choice to listen to your soul NOW, so you don't wake up one day regretting what you missed along the way! *Embrace opportunities NOW instead of waiting for that "perfect moment."* Live with enthusiasm, and never forget: No one can do that for you. It's a gift you give yourself.

It's application time again!

Please take out your notebook and get ready for a **"Seize the Moment" exercise.**

> *Write down all the things you could do, beginning today, to feel alive and excited about your life!*

Generate a sense of vitality from within. *Consider all the actions, interactions, and acknowledgments which could generate a passion for life!* Generating positive momentum is vitally important to remaining "in the flow" of your creative potential. Meaningful, soul-driven transformations need consistent positive action to align yourself with a new, expansive consciousness.

> *Thinking and dreaming alone won't bring you closer to feeling peace or creating joy, success, and fulfillment in your life. Change requires inspired positive action inspired by your spirit.*

Your energy changes when you seize opportunities, allowing new flows of inspiration to saturate your entire being!

Your "seize the moment" list should be ever-expanding. Add to it each day or create a new list each morning! This is a very empowering and exciting way to begin each day.

Here are some "seize the moment" activities you can apply in your own life. *The options for being in the NOW are infinite.* They can be as simple as you like. Just promise yourself to apply one of them (or one of your own!) each day.

Write a letter.
Start a gratitude list.
Turn on some music and dance.
Burst out singing.
Stop to smell the roses. Really.
Laugh. Then laugh some more.

Talk a "gratitude" walk.

Throw a party for no reason.

Meditate and focus on your breath.

Capture the moment by taking a photograph.

Paint. Let your creativity flow.

Create a vision board.

Do some gardening.

Splash in the pool.

Soak in the bathtub.

Gaze at the stars in the night sky.

Pack a picnic basket and bask in the sun.

Clear the clutter in one room of your home.

Pamper yourself with a massage.

Buy a new book.

Plant some flowers.

Listen to inspiring music.

Compose a song or poetry.

Start a creative project.

Begin writing a blog.

Smile at a stranger.

Exercise. Move your body.

Play in the rain.

Slow down to notice the beauty around you.

Look into the eyes of your pet.

Play your favorite musical instrument.

Call a friend to chat.

Create a photo album.

Do something entirely unexpected for someone.

Tell someone you love him or her.

Send flowers to someone (even yourself.)

Appreciate nature. Go sit outside.

Set a positive intention for your day.

Enjoy the sunrise or sunset.

Give a compliment with a smile.

Breathe deeply for 1 minute.

Jump for joy for no reason.
Write and mail a handwritten letter.
Give someone a hug.
Ask for forgiveness.
Extend forgiveness.
Thank someone for being in your life.
Indulge in your favorite food or drink.
Visit or call a loved one in need.
Buy a journal and express your dreams.
Listen when someone else is talking.
Hold your partner's hands unexpectedly.
Sign up for a dance or exercise class.
Go for a long drive.
Light a candle. Make a wish.
Volunteer at a hospital or animal shelter.
Celebrate your unique gifts.
Allow the sunshine to melt away your stress.

Begin by feeling what you wish to experience. Be fully present and engaged in your intentions and activities. Notice the opportunities for connection and love which exist all around you. Open your spiritual eyes to pay attention to the sights, sounds, and beauty surrounding you. Give thanks for these blessings.

> *Approach this new way of living in the moment with a renewed sense of appreciation and gratitude. It won't be very rewarding if you do it out of guilt, frustration or desperation!*

Lead from your soul. Seize your creative power to realize the joy available to you as you become "present" in the present.

Joy is all around, waiting to be acknowledged! You are worthy of this. I set an intention each morning before I even get out of bed. *I set the intention to claim the joy available to me in each and every moment.* It may sound silly, but it works! You can experience bliss, prosperity, and inner peace if you choose to attract them. This is your birthright. It begins by shifting your outlook, expanding your perspective, and tapping into the fertile soil of your consciousness. Simply set a daily intention to be open to the flow (giving and receiving) of love, abundance and JOY. Once you've done that, focus on taking moment-to-moment actions that support your intention! "Success" and "happiness" are completely within your reach... just beyond the boundaries of your old limiting patterns.

> *Soul success is not an end result.*
> *It consists of small day to day*
> *and moment to moment victories of the soul.*
> *It is felt and known in each moment.*

Creating change has only one overriding requirement: making pro-active, conscious decisions on a daily and moment to moment basis. This awareness opens new doors. The moments in which you align your soul with your thoughts, feelings, and actions are the times you create the most powerful results. Live in the energy of your desires NOW! Don't wait to feel fulfilled or successful in the future.

What can you do today to generate positive results from your experiences? **One simple, deliberate choice can lead to a profoundly different outcome.**

Ask yourself these questions throughout the day:

- ⅄ What can I do to keep the momentum of JOY flowing?
- ⅄ Am I contributing to the creation of greater harmony or greater chaos right now?
- ⅄ Do I have a clearly focused intention?
- ⅄ Is it bringing me greater peace?
- ⅄ It is allowing for deeper and closer connection with my loved ones?
- ⅄ Does it contribute to my overall success and happiness?

⅄   Or, am I impulsively reacting to people and situations from habit, when I should be consciously responding from spirit?

The answers to those questions will reveal the effectiveness of your present choices and actions.

> *Intentional living brings lightness to the flow.*
> *Auto-pilot living repeats old limiting patterns*
> *and brings heaviness and tension.*
> *You always have the opportunity to choose again!*

You can always make a new choice. Infuse the energy of love and peace into your thoughts, actions and words. Lead with your soul.

Realizing your soul's potential to create beautiful, empowering shifts in your life involves small daily steps to elevate your energy and direct it towards your dreams. Seize each beautiful moment as a gift! *Avoid being overwhelmed. Major goals and intentions can be broken down into bite-size mini intentions, and addressed one step at a time. The key is taking small day to day steps,* allowing the process of growth and change to become less daunting AND more fun. Maintain a child-like sense of enthusiasm about your life, making your day to day progress fun and playful!

"Carpe Momento" is remembering what you love doing, then putting your heart and soul into it. It requires making a valuable contribution to your own well being on a daily basis. In doing so, you will naturally contribute to the well being of those around you. When you live "on purpose" by tapping into your creative power, the efforts made towards your expansion are not only worthwhile, they are joy-FULL and soul-FULL.

You can begin these small steps toward your expansion by a simple commitment to yourself right now. Will you say "yes?"

Would you be willing to:

- ⚔ Recognize your soul's true mission is simply to BE your authentic self, BE happy, and CLAIM your infinite creative potential?
- ⚔ Realize you don't need to be "fixed" because you aren't "broken?"
- ⚔ Accept personal responsibility to live each day with a sense of purpose?
- ⚔ Stay focused on the present instead of living in the past or the future?
- ⚔ Listen, learn and allow novel perspectives to shed light on new ways to experience life and relationships?
- ⚔ Become aware of new opportunities?
- ⚔ And... stop procrastinating. Move beyond your fears one step at a time?

There is no such thing as failure.
There are only actions and consequences.

Everyone makes mistakes, but awakened souls know they are opportunities to learn and expand. Challenges lead to spiritual growth, healing and expansion.

You are ready to step into your creative power. ***There are no coincidences in life, only divinely designed moments for expansion. It's time to notice these opportunities.*** What would you like to experience? What are you ready to let go of? Are you inspired, energized, and motivated? If not, what could you do to create greater inspiration in your life? Are you making daily strides toward realizing your dreams? Are you embracing each moment as an opportunity to experience yourself anew?

Beginning today, experience the power of each precious moment by embracing the "Carpe Momento" way of being. Begin taking those small steps which allow you to experience greater joy and harmony. The external world will follow suit!

Go out and make it a great day for yourself. Do something that makes you feel alive. ***Do something you truly WANT to do, not just those things you SHOULD do.***

If you knew you were going to be leaving this world soon and had only one phone call to make, who would you call? What would you say? Why are you waiting? How would you spend your time? Which activities and experiences would bring you the greatest joy and fulfillment?

SEIZE THE MOMENT!

PART II
Conscious Living

10. WHAT IS SYNCHRONICITY?

Embracing our creative power begins with awareness. As we cultivate trust in our inner guidance system, we understand our souls' constant attempt to set the direction of our journeys. ***You are reading these words at this moment because your soul led you to them.*** You acted on an internal nudging and followed a signal that led you to this moment. I call this "synchronicity!"

Learning about synchronicity is like putting on 3-D glasses to see new dimensions reveal themselves in your day-today experiences.

Those dimensions have been there all along, but now you are aware of them. Once you know what synchronicity is and how to look for it, you will begin to notice it everywhere!

It happens to people all the time. Something prompts you to look at the clock at exactly the same time of day or night—1:11, 3:33, 4:44. You ponder a challenging situation and hear a song's lyrics that provide an instant solution. You think of someone just before that person contacts you. Or, you read an article, get into your car, see the numbers and letters on the license plate in front of you reflecting the subject of the article you've just finished reading about.

Synchronicities are the result of a deep and profound connection between infinite universal intelligence and our physical realm. But, this connection often defies our traditional sense of logic! Synchronicity reminds us that these perfectly choreographed events do not happen randomly.

Uncovering the meaning behind these events often defies the rational mind, but once beyond the mind, "miracles" happen.

"Synchronicity" is divinely designed signs offered by the soul to guide our daily decisions and responses, allowing us the greatest opportunity for harmonious expansion. Paying attention to these signs affords us the opportunity to move through our journeys in harmony with our souls. **Synchronicity appears magical, yet it's the most natural expression of the universe affirming our deepest desires and requests.** It is revealed through signs and signals placed in our path to guide us in these physical bodies.

When we notice a deeper meaning behind the seemingly random moments in our lives, we naturally expand the possibilities available to us. We give ourselves a new perspective, a grander one than we've allowed ourselves to acknowledge before.

Powerful and divinely inspired inner workings happen beneath the surface of the physical universe. **Synchronicity is expressed through sudden insights affirming answers to our deepest questions.** These insights steer us in the direction of our souls' highest expression, where we engage in an ever-present dance of energy past the signposts in our path. These experiences were designed by our eternal selves and can be seen as parallel events.

Events in the outer world parallel forces in our inner world.
They are a signature of divine orchestration,
a convergence of spirit and matter.

Within us is a wise sage, the source of all wisdom, attempting to guide us by the power of synchronicity. You may identify with your body and personality, but you are far grander than the shell you appear to be. ***Beyond the mortal boundaries of your physical form, you are an eternal being. Within you lies a chamber containing infinite wisdom.*** You can tap into this limitless reservoir of information by noticing, trusting and acting on the signs that appear before you each day at synchronistic moments.

With awareness and desire, you will receive these insights from your soul through subtle sight, sound, and sensing. ***Open yourself to fascinating new vistas of consciousness by connecting to the brilliant counselor within.*** Never again rely on anything outside yourself to determine your path or provide you with validation or approval. All your answers reside within, revealing themselves externally with greater frequency as you pay attention to their subtle guidance.

Signs come to you in one of six ways: sight, sound, taste, smell, feeling, or involuntary body movement. These signs are being communicated by your "inner guru". The intuitive messages are divinely inspired. They answer a question, guide you in a particular direction, or offer specific knowledge applicable to a current situation.

> ***When you pay attention and expect synchronistic moments, you leave behind "luck" and "coincidence" and notice the inspired opportunities your soul places in your path.***

To heal yourself, your relationships, and the planet, the greatest thing you can do is trust yourself. Be open to the infinite sage within, who is always attempting to keep your life on track. Notice the signs! The idea of being guided by synchronicity may seem illogical or mysterious, yet it is your God-given right to follow your inner guidance as often as possible.

Choose the path of least resistance by following the signals and signs of your soul. Everyone has access to this inspiration. Now is your opportunity to claim your "inner guru", notice its brilliant wisdom, and allow it to lead the way. This is what it means to "lead with your soul." *What once seemed out of your control will change immediately as you consciously respond to life by following the guidance offered of your soul.*

A common hurdle to experiencing synchronicity is the mistake of applying *literal* interpretation to the *not-so-literal* synchronistic events in your life. Synchronicites are multi-dimensional, so *these messages need to be interpreted symbolically rather than literally.* View these divine signs from the perspective of the soul instead of interpreting meaning from a physical perspective. For example, if you have a dream about getting married and then meet an attractive person the same day, the underlying synchronistic message is that you are integrating new and attractive qualities into yourself. A physical world interpretation might cause you to falsely interpret the message by believing you should *literally* ask that person to marry you! Do not misinterpret synchronistic moments by giving them a literal meaning.

Synchronicity is often confused with mere coincidence, but this confusion demeans the divinely inspired messages with cynicism and doubt. *Coincidental experiences are random, chance events with no purpose or meaning behind their timing or reason.* Our scientific world view is built on the concept of cause and effect, so we doubt and deny aspects of experience that aren't measurable and verifiable. So, when particular events coincide in startling ways, the first words we might hear or say are, "Oh, it's just a coincidence" or "That was weird!"

When synchronistic moments occur people overlook the deeper meaning when they say, "I got lucky", or "Wow, that happened just in the nick of time", "It came out of the blue", or "The idea just jumped out at me". Nothing ever appears "out of the blue." Our experiences are reflections of the vibrations we emit. Furthermore, *all we experience gains meaning only by our perception of it. As we expand our perception, we expand its meaning,* so experiences become far more purposeful.

Synchronicity is also different from serendipity. Serendipity is generally defined as "accidental good fortune," such as when you are looking for something in a drawer and find something else you had long been looking for. Synchronicity is also distinctly different from premonitions, when one has a hunch or insight that comes to pass. In these cases, one is simply experiencing insights about a future event.

> *Synchronicity isn't random.*
> *There is a purposeful connection between events*
> *that may very well look like*
> *coincidences, serendipities, or premonitions on the surface.*

As we expand our perspective to reflect an interpretation aligned with our soul (instead of the personality alone), we will experience the divinely designed rewards of synchronicity.

Carl Jung, the Swiss psychiatrist who coined the term and brought the phenomenon to light, recognized that synchronicity (which he defined as meaningful coincidence) had the effect of breaking through the "rationalistic shell" of the modern scientific mind. He described it as a form of coincidence powerful enough to shatter the notion that material science has discovered all there is to know about the universe. To the person experiencing synchronicity, *the realization dawns that a mysterious force is at play in the world—a kind of "cosmic clock" whose gears operate on a more subtle plane*. Jung's discovery of synchronicity is to psychology what Einstein's discovery of the law of relativity in physics.

Modern science measures and validates the relationship between cause and effect in the dimensions of time and space. What fascinated

Jung about synchronicity was its "acausal" nature. He defined it as an "acausal relationship of events," with no apparent explanation for the occurrence of two simultaneous events, one subjective and one objective. Further adding to the mystery, he noted that the occurrence has special meaning for the person who experiences it. This implies that **unknown forces in our universe have the capacity to give concrete form to the contents of the invisible realm of consciousness.**

Jung's pioneering exploration of the phenomenon of synchronicity appears to have been an extraordinary synchronicity itself with regard to the development of human consciousness. His first writings on the subject were published in the 1950's, a significant period in the evolution of consciousness, when people around the world started having experiences surpassing the limits of the rational mind. His ideas on synchronicity added fuel to the revolution in consciousness that exploded in the 1960's, when growing numbers of educated people began to glimpse (whether through spiritual methods or psychopharmacological drugs) invisible dimensions of reality. By the 1970s, the idea of synchronicity worked its way into films and novels, and by the 80s, into popular music and games.

Later, in 1993, the topic of synchronicity was catapulted even further into mass consciousness in the novel *The Celestine Prophecy.* **Author James Redfield revealed that all coincidences are significant because they point the way to an unfolding of our personal destinies.** The extraordinary global success of this book revealed our deep attachment to synchronistic experiences. The first of the book's nine "Insights," described the fundamental process of spiritual evolution and explained the importance of meaningful coincidences. He wrote: "The First Insight is a reconsideration of the inherent mystery that surrounds our individual lives on this planet. We are experiencing these mysterious coincidences, and even though we don't understand them yet, we know they are real. We are sensing again, as in childhood, that there is another side of life that we have yet to discover, some other process operating behind the scenes."

For many awakening souls, synchronicity provides a direct and undeniable encounter with the mysterious realm of spirit. These experiences have specific meanings to each individual, and contain the power to open a portal to the infinite wisdom of our souls. Through the convergence of our internal and external realms—in time and space—a thinning of the veil occurs for the person experiencing synchronicity.

> *An opening into the soul and the invisible dimensions*
> *of the universe suddenly appears as the veil between*
> *heaven and earth thins to nothingness.*

Although some synchronistic events, like instant intuitions, cannot be easily ignored, others are far more subtle — almost dreamlike in their metaphorical patterns — and it takes awareness and practice to notice and decode them. *Our belief systems often dictate how we perceive synchronicity.* When this occurs, a person may attribute positive happenings to luck, fate, destiny, karma, or even a miracle. But, as we broaden our perspective, these divine gifts from the soul can be recognized and celebrated! It is far more enjoyable living life in the driver's seat of our existence. *We aren't just pawns on the chessboard of life! We can't wait for "luck" to determine our experience;* we must embrace divine guiding as we consciously create our experience from moment to moment.

When we live with conscious awareness and deliberate attention to the signs and signals along our path, we step into empowered living. With disciplined focus, we start to notice opportunities we didn't see before! If our thoughts revolve around what we lack, we will not see these synchronistic opportunities appear in our lives.

> *An open heart and an open mind will*
> *maximize synchronistic moments!*
>
> *Expect great things to happen, and the*
> *universe will open doors for you.*

> ***Be alert, aware, and ready to take action
> when positive opportunities come your way.***

Recognize the synchronistic matrix of your experience, and you will be empowered as a creative, co-operative and active partner in your own awakening and expansion! The more open you are to synchronicity, the more it occurs. The extent to which you recognize the dreamlike nature of your waking universe determines the degree to which your life will be synchronistic. Once you become aware of your own waking dream, and recognize that you live in a synchronistic universe, your world will shape itself according to your awareness.

Synchronicity holds the divine power to heighten your memory of the higher dimensions of consciousness. When these unusual experiences occur, you examine your physical reality from a more subtle plane of existence. When these events occur in your life repeatedly and with growing frequency, you realize that an invisible, intelligent force (the divinity within you) is trying to attract your attention! You are reminded that this divine energy is actively thinning the veil between spirit and matter—but only when you are open and responsive. ***The phenomenon of synchronicity guides your journey by helping you resonate with the vibration of your soul.***

It's application time!

Please take out your notebooks and title this exercise:

DETECTING SYNCHRONICITY IN MY LIFE.

Whether in special or mundane circumstances, ***synchronicity appears in many forms. It can be as dramatic as a firecracker or as subtle as the passing of a breeze across your cheek.*** You instantly interpret its meaning or its significance may leave you utterly baffled. A synchronisitic event can change your life or pass you by, leaving no trace of a memory.

To understand how synchronicity manifests itself, begin to notice the different patterns in which it appears: single synchronicities; strings of synchronicities that emphasize a single point; and purpose-full, multi-layered synchronicity clusters.

Over the course of your day, begin to notice these patterns. As you become aware of these experiences the light of truth will shine on your multi-dimensional journey! You will surprise and delight yourself with the magic occurring all around you.

You will begin to celebrate this new-found awareness as a gift from your soul, offering you a map for the gentle yet powerful unfolding of your divine destiny.

SINGLE SYNCHRONICITIES

These are the simplest, most direct expressions of synchronicity. A single synchronicity has a beginning, a middle, and an end, and it stands out from ordinary day-to-day experiences. For example, you are at the grocery store, and cross paths with a friend you haven't seen in years. You do a double-take, stop and have a brief conversation, say good-bye, and continue shopping. *What makes this encounter a synchronicity? The coinciding of inner and outer events which cannot be explained by cause and effect, but is still meaningful to the one experiencing the event.* You did nothing to arrange the meeting with your friend and had no idea she was even in town. Perhaps you were thinking of her recently, for the first time in years. Your thoughts of her would be the inner event, and the physical meeting the outer event. The meaning might be in the wonder you feel at how things are connected. Or, perhaps she fills a need for you. Maybe you've been considering a career change, and it turns out she recently started a new business in the field you are interested in! Your thoughts about your desired career change are the inner event, the meeting and her information about her new company comprise the outer event, and the meaning might be that now is the time to take the plunge into your new career. Or, perhaps you've been trying to experience your life more consciously, at deeper levels. In this case, your aspirations are the inner event, the meeting the outer event, and its significance to you is that you're on the right track!

Without seeing this event as a synchronicity, meeting your friend would be "just a coincidence," with no meaning whatsoever for you. You would see nothing special about bumping into her and make nothing of it. The unlikely encounter wouldn't lead you anywhere— not to inward searching, not to a decision to change careers, nor to the power of conscious living.

> *Single synchronicities often occur as telephone calls, chance encounters, or lucky numbers.*

Information you need might come your way via some surprising route, just at the moment you need it. Just because a single synchronicity is simple in pattern doesn't mean it can't have a great impact on your life. ***Looking back on your life, you might find that a turning point, such as meeting your significant other, was a single synchronicity.***

SYNCHRONICITY STRINGS

Synchronicity strings happen one after the other, as though a point is being reiterated. Perhaps the friend you bumped into at the grocery store was a college classmate you used to go dancing with. Later that day, you hear a song on the radio that reminds you of old college party days! Then, several days later, you turn on the television to see a movie trailer with an actress who has the same first name as the friend you bumped into. That would be a string of synchronicities. Depending on your current circumstances, there could be a variety of meanings. Perhaps it brings the lack of fun in your life into focus, clarifying what you need more of. It might bring a realization that you've spent years ignoring your deep passion for dance while working at a job you can't stand. You might notice a fantastic opportunity to change careers and work as a dance instructor at your friends new business!

It is the sequence of occurrences that make this a string of synchronicities. Meeting your friend at the store after so many years might be coincidence to some; hearing an old song on the radio or a name on television might be something more. But, *because all of these events occur one after another, their totality resonates in your consciousness with specific meaning to you.*

Repeating numbers or words are another way you might notice strings of synchronicities in your life. A certain number may start to emerge as a signal of something important. You may never have heard a word or phrase before, and then you'll hear it several times, in different forms and contexts. Sometimes the connection between your life and the number sequence or phrase is clear and direct; sometimes it's a puzzle. For example, a number sequence holding deep significance for me, revealing I am "on path", is my daughter's birth month and day (1124),and her time of birth (1153). When I flow with life rather than resist it, I notice those number on my clock every single day. It's a great synchronicity which repeatedly affirms my alignment with my soul. It is a daily gift, inspiring me to remain in the flow!

Strings of synchronicities might also reveal themselves through the repeated intersection or parallels between you and another person. For example, perhaps someone you knew from grade school ends up living across the street from you as an adult, in a completely different city than where you both grew up! Then, you discover your spouses worked in the same building for 10 years after college! Next, you discover your children went to the same high school at different times AND that you both have golden retriever dogs! Begin to notice if anything like this happens to you!

PURPOSE-FULL SYNCHRONICITY CLUSTERS

A synchronicity cluster is similar to a synchronicity string in that it ***involves a series of linked synchronicities, but its pattern is richer and far more complex:*** It involves many different types of synchronicity with ***multiple layers and levels of meaning*** that coalesce over time around a particular theme. Out of a cluster, you draw not just a single message or direction, but a broader and deeper understanding of a basic dynamic in your life's journey.

For example, let's go back to the store where you ran into your old friend. You're amazed to see her there, and the coincidence is even more astonishing because she's only in that part of town for a meeting. She invites you to join her and some friends for dinner that night. You just happen to be free because a few minutes earlier, your child's parent/teacher conference was canceled. Struck by the timing, you say "yes!" You don't mind being away from home for the evening because you'd had words with your spouse the night before regarding your child's university preference.

At dinner that night, it turns out your friend's two friends are college professors. You realize this is an opportunity to gain information you can bring home to enlighten your spouse. You bring up the topic of in state and out of state colleges. As they launch into a discussion of the differences, you realize they're mirroring your disagreement with your spouse from the night before. One of them says a phrase over and over that really hits you: "Let's get to the heart of the matter." You try to figure out why you feel tense, but then you recall your father used to say those exact words to your mother when they were fighting. In fact, you notice the man's name, Larry, is the same as your father's. It brings memories of how much you hated hearing your parents argue—and you begin to wonder how much of your parents' dynamic is affecting your current relationship. But as the two talk, you see something remarkable happening: they come to common ground, a realization of how they're bonded by the impact of their teaching experiences. On the way home, the radio announcer says, "Home is where the heart is," a phrase you haven't heard in years, and you consider its meaning regarding relationships, especially your own. It makes you sentimental and when you arrive home, you're no longer angry.

Let's look at the cluster of synchronicities here: the significant encounter, the timely cancellation, the mirrored argument, the repeated phrase. *These could all appear singly or in a string, but when they appear in a cluster, they are particularly insightful and revealing.* The overall theme revealed here is conflict. Jungians might say your disagreement from the night before aroused in your psyche a need for a deeper understanding of the issue, and that this generated the energy that caused you to attract the synchronicities. You can derive many meanings from the cluster, including your desire for greater conflict resolution.

The more deeply you notice and understand synchronicity, the more you will be able to see the myriad ways that your soul is attempting to communicate with you.

The goal? Purposeful expansion and conscious living! Awaken your innate ability to unravel the meaning of the synchronistic patterns in your own life and surroundings. When you detect synchronistic events around you, the benefits are monumental!

You can directly participate in the unfolding of your divine destiny and the manifestation of synchronistic phenomena through vigilance and focused attention. What's more empowering than realizing your power to be the conscious creator of your life experience? Synchronistic events will be attracted according to the way you expect them.

Shakespeare said all the world is a stage, and this is literally true. Reality is intentionally created.
Every event–no matter how small or vast in scale, whether momentary or the culmination of millions of years of unseen causes and effects, is attracted by the energy you emit.

We are the on-stage actors, but we have become so absorbed in our parts that we forget we are on our very own stage. *It's time to awaken! Here. Now. Awaken to the awareness that you are on your self-created stage.* Some of the other actors around you may proceed through their lives in a semi-trancelike state, but you have awakened to a highly engineered reality, similar to the holodecks of Star Trek or the computer-generated realities of "The Matrix" movies!

You are free to act-out your personal drama as you please. The beauty of understanding synchronicity is realizing you are not alone on stage, having to direct, produce and star in the production all by yourself! There is a stage crew, people working behind the scenes to keep the play going smoothly. This ever-supportive energetic crew helps you by arranging all the events and circumstances of your life. *You are the actor, and your (divine) production crew uses the unseen extra dimensions to arrange the synchronicities that give meaning to your production!* Most actors around you never come out of character to even notice the stage crew. They take matters unfolding in their plays very seriously, but are unaware of the support they receive in arranging their reality.

You, on the other hand, are now conscious, and know your personal stage crew is ready to arrange events for you to help in your chosen plot. Who are these crew members? Just souls like yourself, but residing in the invisible realms waiting to lend a hand. Now that you know they are involved, you can converse with them through the synchronistic events they create. They communicate with you not only through events, but through other actors who remain consciously unaware of this stage crew.

Now you are aware, so *look for synchronistic events indicating signals from the stage crew!* Have fun with this new empowering information and allow it to add more color, vibrancy, interest and passion to your journey. Life is meant to be FUN. Allow synchronicity to add that FUN!

11. AWARENESS

Life can be uninspired and mundane, OR it can be a joyful adventure! Awareness plays a significant role in determining the quality of our lives. As creative beings, we generate momentum with every thought, emotion, and expectation. Oftentimes, we do this by default – without awareness.

To create "heaven on earth", we must first expand our awareness to fully understand the scope of our creative powers.

Otherwise, we simply react to life instead of purposefully generating a positive flow of energy to create success from the inside-out.

We are alive to embrace a journey of self-discovery. **In this journey, we are intended to take responsibility for our creations. We are intended to claim creative control.** When this happens, we are empowered. We stop blaming other people or external circumstances for our feelings and reactions. With awareness, we remember (from our soul's broader perspective) that nothing outside us holds the power to activate negative emotion or illicit fear _within_ us. This realization offers the greatest sense of liberation available to us as human beings.

Self- knowledge, self-regulation and self-direction are the foundational structure of our ever-expanding spiritual development. Self awareness is the primary building block in generating physical, mental, emotional and spiritual harmony. Our experiences are simply reflections of what we choose to focus on, so we gain immense personal power through heightened awareness. **The more self-aware** *we become, the more we deliberately choose to be proactive instead of reactive.* We recommit to positive change by shedding our unconscious self-sabotaging behaviors!

> *Transcending self-sabotaging behaviors is*
> *the primary goal of expansion.*

But, it requires an awareness of what those behaviors ARE to move beyond them.

The following list includes the primary signs of Self-Sabotaging Behaviors. Notice if you experience of any them.

1. Focusing on what is not working or not right.

This serves as a roadblock because anytime you think or speak about what is going wrong, you feel frustrated and dissatisfied. This can squash your innate sense of inspiration, purpose and ambition.

Action step: Ask yourself a new question: "What's going right?" or "What IS working?" Keep an evidence journal and each day write down everything, I do mean everything, that is working. Change your focus!

2. Feeling stuck in fear.

When you worry about the future or fret about potential negative outcomes, you become paralyzed. From this space, you take no action.

Action step: Place you attention in the present moment without bringing your old stories and fears into your current situation. You simply cannot control other people or outside situations. All you can control is your own vibration. Relax, breathe and trust that the Universe will take care of you – it always does.

3. Feeling you have no value.

Do you forget all your accomplishments and or disregard your unique abilities? If you stew and obsess about the past or your lack of success or lack of goal achievement, you'll be stuck in a debilitating state of lack. If you often criticize yourself or can't accept compliments, it's time to bump of the self-love meter.

Action step: When you hear your that gremlin voice inside yourself reminding you of what you haven't done right or well, turn down the volume and turn UP the volume to your true self -- the one that knows the TRUTH about who you are and how you add immense value to the world. Acknowledge at least 5 things every day that you did well. Compliment yourself on something you did that you feel good about. Celebrate the small successes!

4. Comparing yourself to others.

Do you constantly compare yourself to others and then feel negatively about yourself when compared to them? Comparison doesn't motivate us to do more or be better, instead it makes us feel we'll never be good enough and we aren't right now.

Action step: When you find yourself back in comparison game, notice how similar you are with the other person vs. what is different. Create a list of 25 adjectives that describe your greatness. Whenever you notice yourself in a comparison mode, think of some of the adjectives that describe YOU.

5. Meeting goals and then sabotaging your success.

Do you not believe that you deserve to accomplish goals and receive the fruits of your labor? What is the underlying story you tell yourself? Do you feel unworthy of having success?

Action step: List 5 recent accomplishments. How did they make you feel?

6. Chasing away relationships.

Do you always feel something is missing in your relationships or find fault with the other person? Perhaps you are afraid of intimacy. Underneath this is usually a fear of abandonment or exposure that causes you to distance yourself from others.

Action step: Create a list of the qualities you value in a relationship and the qualities you want to attract in your partners. Cultivate those qualities in yourself! Focus on what you want instead of what you fear.

By developing greater awareness, you will learn to pause before you speak and act. You learn to rein in your impulsiveness to create your life on purpose! With awareness, you clearly define your intentions and identify your desires, paving the way for a rewarding, fulfilling life! *Personal responsibility and accountability empower you to create the future of your dreams, moment by moment, instead of waiting for "fate" to determine your experiences.* Randomness, determinism and coincidence become obsolete concepts.

Self-awareness opens the door to unlimited power.

It is time for a consciousness make-over. It is time to invoke the agent of change called self-awareness to let go of old, toxic perspectives preventing you from designing a lifestyle rooted in the desires and dreams of your soul. *Soul-inspired solutions are discovered with expanded awareness.*

The journey into greater self-awareness involves your ability to assess your life without any attachment to it being right or wrong, good or bad. This happens as you view your life as though you were watching a movie, looking at your experiences from the vantage point of a neutral observer to gain a new perspective. Your old perspective stands in the way of your desired future. So, as you shift the way you see yourself, others, and the world, imagine the shifts you could make and the things you could create!

A state of non-judgment will allow you to create the future you desire and deserve. A new perspective will quiet your mind and open new doors of possibility.

To gain clarity about your current state of consciousness,
answer the following questions.

- "What decisions have I made recently that feel aligned with my soul?"
- "What limiting assumptions have I drawn about my life that keep me stuck repeating the past?"
- "What beliefs do I continue to carry that drain my life force and rob me of my desired future?"
- "What do I consistently *say* to myself throughout the day that keeps any negativity alive in my energy field?"
- "What is one action I could take today that would bring me closer to living the life I dream of? Schedule a time to take the action today.
- What thought could I think today that would evoke the feelings I want to experience most? Think that thought today.

Integrating greater personal awareness into your daily life will dramatically impact the quality of your experiences. Awareness offers practical benefits that will powerfully support you in every area of life. Although this may seem an abstract concept, its underlying power is far-reaching and profoundly significant for anyone who wishes to consciously create their own experience. *You will navigate your way through life far more effectively when you harness the power of personal awareness!*

Expanding your personal awareness will broaden your vision, heighten your senses, and give greater meaning and purpose to your daily life. Your perspective will change to allow a greater flow of joy, prosperity, and harmony. This inner focus will cultivate a deeper connection with your soul and empower you to create your life more deliberately than ever before.

> *Self reflection is at the root of awareness.*
> *Ask yourself: Where is my attention focused now?*

Begin observing your focus with greater regularity. As you train yourself to notice your attention shifts, it will become easier to consciously direct it.

"*Where your attention goes, energy flows.*" Deliberate focus inspires greatness, allowing you see and feel glimpses of your spiritual self beyond the physical body. Tap into this kind of inspiration by projecting your attention deliberately.

Don't fixate on what's wrong in your life because it blocks the flow of inspiration. Choose to become more aware, clear the inner clutter, and allow the fullness of your spiritual self to come through. *The less attention you give to explaining why you don't feel well, the quicker you will shift into feeling better again!*

The goal of expanding our awareness is greater harmony in our communication and interactions. Negative habits like venting our frustration only generate greater discord in our lives. Venting is helpful only when we express what we want more of – more connection, more peace, more joy, more love. When we "vent" with the purpose of justifying our position or to prove others wrong, we only amplify our frustration. So, *express yourself in empowering ways that reflect your desires – and not your criticism.*

It's application time again!

Please take out your notebooks and title this exercise:

Awareness = Power : Maintaining a High Frequency Life

Time to make a few choices. Review the questions and reflect on your answers. The questions are intended to stimulate your awareness and offer you the option to make new choices. Journal the responses that make you feel expansive!

Am I identifying with my limited self or my infinite self?

Is my heart open and available to love right now or is my heart closed?

Am I saying "YES" or "NO" to the daily gifts of expansion available to me?

Am I open to the sacredness and beauty of the moment or are am busy finding fault?

Am I focused on what I have to lose or what I have to gain?

How can I expand my perspective to allow for new outcomes?

How can I become a more confident version of myself and make decisions with clarity?

Am I willing to let go of all judgments of myself and others that are holding me back?

Am I ready to see that challenges are blessings in disguise?

Will I choose to expand or contract right now?

Am I navigating with optimism or pessimism?

Am I stretching to meet life on a higher plateau or shrinking back into my shell?

Am I tapping into my creativity or suppressing it?

Am I choosing love or fear more consistently?

Can I let go of worries to explore my future with positive expectancy?

Can I expand my views and beliefs to see life through a broaden lens?

Will I allow my truth to be acknowledged and illuminated?

Do I see life through a broad cosmic lens or through the narrow lens of the ego?

Am I allowing my essence to be revealed in my relationships?

Am I available for new opportunities or am I sabotaging them?

Am I being authentic in my day-to-day life, or hiding behind a false ego-driven mask to please others ?

Will I discover JOY in as many moments as possible today?

Will I embrace the present by releasing the past?

Will I make new choices to allow for better results?

Are my choices aligned with my ego or my soul?

Am I striving for connection or seeking reasons to feel separate from others?

Am I focused on what I am grateful for or on what's missing in my life?

Do I spend more time nurturing or criticizing myself?

Are my beliefs causing me to expand or contract in my daily experiences?

Am I standing in my own way by not acknowledging my unique brilliance ?

Will I trade toxicity for peace?

Will I let go of patterns and beliefs that no longer serve me, so I can express my pure potential?

Isn't it time to celebrate my unique genius and creative power?

Remember...
You can make a change right now.

It's your option.

You're at a crossroads. Will you
choose expanded awareness?

12. INNER COMPASS

There are two questions you need to ask yourself today:

**"Which direction will bring me one step closer
to fulfilling my Sacred Purpose for EXPANSION?"**

And

**"Which choice will LEAD ME ONE STEP FORWARD
on the divinely designed pathway for my SOUL?"**

The answers will come from your inner compass.

You have an internal GPS to help you navigate life. Do you feel its guidance? Do you hear its silent, yet powerful messages? Or, is there too much static to even notice its existence? To connect with your inner compass, practice stillness. Only then will you feel the divine guidance and hear the message.

Look into the mirror of your life and experiences. What do you see reflected there? Do you see Balance? Peace? Harmony? Self love? Acceptance of others? Passion for life? If not, you must extend your vision, expand your awareness to focus on the limitless possibilities for growth. These opportunities appear when you follow your inner compass. Divine guidance is always available.

*Your vision must simply be clear enough to notice doors
opening, and your heart must be peaceful enough to hear
the subtle guidance leading you to those doors.*

Far too often the haze of chaotic living obscures opportunities so you see only closed doors and locked windows. Consciously transcend the confines of ego-centered living, make decisions from your heart, and magnificent doors of opportunity will open with ease.

Look at yourself carefully with your spiritual eyes, not your ego's eyes. Embrace your light, let it shine into the world. Your soul wants to shine! *Listen to your heart, follow your inner compass to walk through divinely designed gateways leading to a powerful, self-directed life*. Ground yourself in your innate strength and authority. Remember you are an immensely powerful spiritual being meant to fulfill your sacred purpose through the process of growth and awakening.

Your inner compass gives directions from your soul, quietly whispering to you every day. Listen to these directions and act on them. You will feel inspired by feelings of serenity, peacefulness, and even relief. *To connect with your soul, you need personal clarity, a keen sense of awareness, and a willingness to act on your intuition each day.* Consciously create a flow of clear, organized energy (through intention, meditation, creativity, imagination and focus). Otherwise, you will be too distracted to notice the subtle voice of your soul as it attempts to reveal the pathway to your sacred, divine purpose.

To clear the internal noise, become aware of the external distractions in your environment that prevent you from experiencing the serenity required to hear the guidance. This liberates you from the inside-out.

What is the correlation between external clutter and internal clarity?
Clutter isn't just about physical excess.
Clutter is anything preventing you from
experiencing the fullness of life.

Clutter is behavioral patterns creating imbalances in your life. Restore balance and you will create vital new energy, passion, and joy in your daily life. Only then will you hear the calls of your inner compass, guiding your journey.

As you clear the space within and around you, you will gently unwind, shedding the layers of your old, tangled self and chaotic former existence. Then you will see the beauty and clarity of your soul. *As you shed the layers of limitation, stagnation and tension, your radiant spirit will shine through.* It takes courage to embark on this adventure, clearing out the cobwebs of your past to unleash your greatest potential. Celebrate your courage and step into the new you!

To purge your life of unnecessary constraints, you must change habits and remove the people and circumstances that no longer serve your soul's goals and desires. It's liberating to clear out the old to make space for the new. *Clear the space around you, and create the space within you for new inspiration, guidance and connection.* You will feel lighter, freer, and more capable of tuning into your inner compass.

Ask yourself:

"If my home and work spaces are outward reflections of my inner self, what do they say about me?"

CLUTTER IS SIMPLY STUCK ENERGY! Energy stagnates when clutter accumulates! You are energetically anchored in your living and working spaces, so when you clear those spaces, you transform your entire life experience. *Everything around you mirrors your inner self.* So, by clearing your external environment, you cleanse your inner self. You will feel lighter, more productive, more energetic and powerful. You deserve this. Remove the clutter and purify the energy in your home, office, car, and life. By transforming your environment, you create clear, open, and receptive channels for love, success, and opportunities.

It's application time!

Please take out your notebooks and title this exercise:

Removing the Clutter!

Start by completely clutter-clearing one room in your home or office. Clear other spaces in your environment when you feel inspired. Clearing out unused or unloved possessions in your home or work environment has an empowering, invigorating effect on your spirit! Spiritual clutter drains you by clogging your energy field and blocking the voice of your intuition. Walk around your house and take a good look at all of your belongings.

Ask yourself:

"What is this saying about me?"

"How is it affecting my energy level?

"Is it creating the effect I want or could I replace it with something better reflecting my inner self?

Let go of anything that drains you. Take the time to walk through every room in your home and look at all of your possessions.

Ask yourself:

"*WHAT DOES THIS SYMBOLIZE TO ME AND HOW DOES IT MAKE ME FEEL?*"

If it isn't uplifting, it's time to release it.

You will feel liberated. ***The cleared space becomes a sanctuary,*** where inspiration flows with ease. Now, create a space that feels beautiful. Add flowers, clean the mirrors, put up inspirational artwork. Rooms can be transformed into spaces of renewal. ***Creating beauty***

and harmony around you promotes internal growth, expansion and renewal.

Please repeat the following affirmations each time you clear a cluttered space:

"I am sweeping away what I don't need to make room for something that enhances my life!"
"There is clarity within me and around me."
"Fresh, invigorating, passionate energy fills my soul."
"As I release what no longer serves me, I create room for limitless love and success."
"My external and internal world are clear. I hear my inner compass."
Remember this motto: "Use it, love it, or get rid of it!"

The goal is to harmonize and balance the flow of energy in your surroundings to create corresponding clarity inside you!

Remember, words have power! Affirming these statements as you clear your spaces speaks directly to your subconscious mind. Clearing clutter in your environment has a powerful corresponding effect on your mental clutter.

Let go of the old to make room for the new, and a new sense of vitality will surge through you!

Enthusiastically celebrate, honoring yourself for all you've released and for the clarity you have gained.

If defining "clutter" is challenging, ask these questions about your possessions:

1. Does this item lift my energy when I look at it?
2. Do I absolutely love it?
3. Is it genuinely useful?

If the answer to each question is not a resounding "YES!", then you are looking at clutter.

Clutter clearing is not only about creating new energetic space. It's about letting go of the past, of old limitations, and fears. It's about achieving clarity of spirit.

This new clarity will make it so much easier to hear your inner compass. Then, simply set the daily intention to nurture your "whole" self by making time for rest, meditation, stretching, exercising, feeling gratitude, play/recreation, and plenty of laughter. *Slow your pace enough to notice the beauty around you and the subtle messages being whispered to you from moment to moment.* Those messages pave the way for a life with purpose, spiritual integrity, and love for all. Closing doors to the past clears energy on many levels , so you can enjoy your day-to-day experiences at a leisurely pace that supports the growth, expansion, and evolution of your soul.

Once the inner static subsides, you will hear and respond to your intuition. You will have the confidence to accept guidance from your inner compass, your higher self. You will expand your vision, hear with new ears, and experience a renewed zest for life flowing from the inside-out.

Remember, a frantic, disorganized environment blocks your inner compass from communicating with you! Internal or external chaos creates emotional turbulence that breaks the connection to your intuitive voice. This is the voice of your soul, and external "noise" prevents you from hearing its guidance. Commit to establishing a renewed clarity. *Release anything preventing you from hearing the clear, confident voice of your soul, then glide onto the path of sacred, purpose-full living.* Every day is a new opportunity to create a fresh existence based on spiritual conviction, courage, love, and self acceptance.

Listen and accept guidance from your internal GPS!
Remain open and receptive.

Listen, trust and act on the subtle, yet powerful guidance of your soul. Move into harmonious, magical living. Actively contribute to your personal growth and be of service to others. Develop the spiritual wings to rise above meaning-less affairs and activities to focus on purpose-full living. Listen to the guidance of your soul, and spiritual rewards will reveal themselves with ease.

Allow your inner compass to direct your
choices, responses and actions.
Create a heavenly paradise on earth.

Are you ready to do YOUR part?

13. YOUR VIBRATIONAL FREQUENCY

So what's all the talk these days about "raising your frequency"? As energetic beings, we all have a frequency. This frequency determines the level of light we emit into the world from our personal energy field. *We can elevate the rate at which our energy field vibrates, which in turn, elevates the quality of our experiences.*

> *Everything in the universe is composed of*
> *vibrating energy, including you.*

Your essence is pure energy, oscillating at a certain frequency. It's likely you've never given much thought to your vibrational frequency before. However, once you understand how it governs your life, it will become a high priority! *Why raise your frequency?* Simply stated, a high vibrational frequency attracts other high frequency (or positive) people, situations and opportunities, while a low vibrational frequency attracts more "negative" situations. You choose the level at which your energy vibrates through the strength and clarity of your thoughts, feelings, and beliefs. The results of your enhanced vibration will be revealed in higher quality experiences.

You can consciously raise the frequencies of your vibration with intention, purpose, and dedication. *Consistency is the key to lasting shifts.* When you do this, you will quickly realize your power to direct your life experience from the inside-out. There is nothing more exciting than tapping into your creative potential and embracing it with a renewed sense of passion and vitality.

Raising your frequency opens you to more opportunities because life simply mirrors your consciousness. The world around you converts your energetic patterns (your thoughts, beliefs, and expectations) into physical reality.

> *Life changes when you recognize your ability to create your own destiny instead of waiting for "luck" to determine your life story.*

You can raise your frequency and shift YOUR personal reality by consciously selecting your thoughts and words. Your self talk is a running dialogue between you and the universe. Become aware of what you say to yourself and what you expect for yourself. For the self-aware, the universe has a funny way of manifesting exactly what we expect!

Without self-awareness, you will attract people and circumstances you don't want in your life! Begin to consciously attract the things you DO want and DO deserve. Consciously shift your focus by placing your awareness on everything you're grateful for, and you will increase your vibration. Shift into an open, receptive frame of mind where beautiful things begin to happen. ***The art of appreciation will transform your life.*** Focus on your blessings, and you will notice yourself becoming even more abundantly blessed with each passing day.

Each challenge is an opportunity to shift reality by consciously raising your vibration instead of reacting in fear. Replace feelings of doubt, stress, guilt, and anger with feelings of peace, acceptance, joy, self-love, and forgiveness. This is always your choice.

You are not a victim of your surroundings unless you choose to be. I say that with respect and love. Shifting your energy field is always a personal choice. Purposefully create your life from the driver's seat of your spiritual vehicle. Take the steering wheel and choose the energy you wish to radiate into the world. The energy you emit determines the circumstances you will attract.

Low vibration means a decreased state of consciousness. As you raise your vibration, you elevate your level of consciousness, opening new possibilities. The more expansive your consciousness, the more expansive your options. *Expand your perspective, align it with your soul, and watch doors swing open as opportunities appear.*

The lower your vibrational frequency, the less you hear the voice of your soul because the turbulence in your energy field drowns out the voice of intuition. Lower frequencies are much denser that higher ones, restricting the flow of divine energy, and impeding the natural flow of your life. *The higher your frequency, the more in tune with life you become, the more you step into the FLOW.* As you align your thoughts, feelings, and actions with your intuitive voice, life becomes more harmonious. Focus on possibilities instead of limitations, and your vibration rises.

> *You cannot focus on negative thoughts or emotions and expect to maintain a high vibration. It's that simple!*

All existence vibrates at unique frequencies. Quantum physics describes the universe as nothing more than vibrating strings of energy. Different parts of your body have their own signatures. The sound of your heart's cells are different from the sound of your lungs cells. *When specific parts of the body become unbalanced, stressed or dis-eased, they are no longer producing harmonious sound waves.* They aren't vibrating at their optimal frequency. To re-calibrate your frequency, and allow your body to shift from dis-ease to harmony and balance, consciously focus on the higher vibrations which produce overall health and vitality.

> *You may be wondering, "how do I know what my vibrational frequency is?"*

This is far simpler than you may think. *You determine the rate of your vibrational frequency by asking yourself how you feel.* It isn't more complicated than that. The better you feel, the higher your frequency; the worse you feel, the lower your frequency. When you vibrate at a high frequency, you attract opportunities, situations, and relationships that perpetuate a wonderful "high" feeling. When you vibrate at a low frequency, you attract people and situations which reinforce a "negative" feeling. *Your feelings inform your intuition, your internal GPS, about the rate of your vibration.*

You will vibrate at different frequencies in different areas of your life. For example, you may have positive thoughts about your health or your relationships, but harbor negative beliefs about money. Your "overall frequency" is an average of how you "vibrate" in all areas of your life.

It's application time!

Please take out your notebook and title this exercise:

WAYS TO INCREASE MY FREQUENCY.

Consider the following ways to increase your rate of vibration and improve your health. Write down the ones that catch your attention and *promise yourself to apply them in your life for the next 21 days. That should be long enough to establish a new, empowering pattern.*

FREQUENCY RAISING TIPS:

Choose an Empowered Vocabulary: Pay close attention the words you use. Refrain from engaging in negative conversations or gossip. These conversations are not productive, and will push your energetic vibration to low levels very quickly. Gossip is the transfer of emotional poison from on person to another. Become aware of whether or not your words are raising or lowering your frequency.

Surround yourself with uplifting people, sounds and surroundings: Don't underestimate the power of listening to music that makes you feel good. Choose to listen to things which have a positive, joyful or relaxing impact on your mood. Your body naturally absorbs sound, which you can liken to a spiritual multi-vitamin: sounds have the power to elevate your mood and re-energize and harmonize your energy field.

Appreciate the Beauty in Nature:. Natural light (sunshine) and pure water raise your vibration! Natural frequencies harmonize with your soul's frequencies. Nurture yourself each day by reconnecting with the earth below you and the trees, flowers and plants around you. Let them ground you. The natural sounds of birds singing and wind moving through the trees helps reduce stress, elevating your vibrational frequency.

Interact with people who lift you higher: Spend time with people who celebrate you, celebrate life, and appreciate the opportunities in each day! Negative people feel tired and drained, and tend to absorb energy from others. When you spend time with positive people, you will feel uplifted and excited about life. This is precisely what increases your frequency!

Commit to CONSCIOUS BREATHING: Focus on your breathing to get centered. Bring in more oxygen to energize your body. Visualize light filling every cell in your body when you inhale, and release any negative thoughts, energies, and stress when you exhale. Repeat as needed until you feel more aligned and peaceful. Throughout the day, when stress rears its head...Pause & Breathe! Take three deep breaths...then let it go!

SLEEP: Your body needs downtime; it requires rest to become revitalized! Dream time is the body's one opportunity to deeply restore, heal and rejuvenate itself. Get plenty of rest so your body naturally raises it's own frequency. Don't underestimate the power of a ten minute nap, or just closing your eyes for a few minutes during your day. Take a break from the "go-go-go" mentality and move in step with the harmony of your spirit. You will emerge with a raised vibration!

EXERCISE: Physical movement not only gets your body's energy flowing, it stimulates the release of endorphins, which elevate your mood, your stress–coping skills AND your frequency. Take a walk, dance or do your favorite workout…just move! As you move your body, stress drains from your energy field. Retaining the dense energy of stress leads to health problems. The root of dis–ease is dense energy. Commit to moving your body, and remain in the flow of harmony, health and peace.

GET CREATIVE! Journaling, painting, cooking, composing music…whatever gets your creative juices flowing and brings you joy, just do it! Tapping into your creativity increases your vibrational frequency because you focus on what inspires you.

EMBRACE THE HEALING POWER OF WATER: Water is a great substance to help raise your frequency. We all know water is essential to physical health, but it's also a powerful aid to your mental, emotional, and spiritual well being. The sound of rain, a waterfall, or a fountain soothes your mind and relaxes your body. You can get a small table-top fountain for about twenty dollars and enjoy the sound of falling water in your home or office. There are also many recordings available of rain, waves, or waterfalls that you can play on your computer or mobile device. The sound of falling water elevates your frequency, allowing you to easily release dense energy.

Spend time soaking in a bath or floating in a pool of water. The water feels gentle and supportive, allowing relaxation to sweep through you. If you don't have the opportunity to soak or float in water, try holding your hands under running water. Pay attention to how the water feels flowing over your hands. Move your hands around in the water and notice the difference between how it feels on the backs of your hands and how it feels on your palms. Hold your hands palms up and slightly cupped, observing how the water forms a little pool. This simple activity focuses you on the present moment and helps release stress, tension and worry.

A shower is a wonderful opportunity to experience the cleansing affects of water not just physically, but emotionally and energetically. Be conscious in the moment when you take your shower. Feel the water pouring over you, caressing your skin. Imagine the water cleansing every cell in your body. Consciously relax your muscles as the water flows over them. Watch the water run down the drain and know it is carrying away not only the dirt, but the dense energy of stress and dis-ease. Feel the lightness of being, liberated from all that density. You may spend a few minutes longer to shower with fully present conscious awareness, but the benefits are worth it. You will feel refreshed both physically and energetically, as you vibrate at a higher frequency.

Drinking water with conscious awareness and appreciation will elevate your frequency, as well. Look at the water in a clear glass or bottle. Notice how clear and simple it is. Bless the water. Let it linger in your mouth before swallowing. Taste it and feel its gentleness. Swallow the water, knowing it is purifying, cleansing and nourishing your body. The water is serving and supporting you. Without it, you would not have life. Feel your gratitude for the water and know that with each sip you are flushing away toxins and revitalizing your entire energy field.

Those are just a few simple tips for raising your vibration and stepping into a higher flow of life, stepping into who you really are! Do this on a consistent basis, and you will notice yourself experiencing the optimal wellness (on every level) you deserve.

Raising your vibrational frequency is a gift you give yourself on a daily basis. Synchronize your frequency with divine light, love, harmony, intention, wisdom and peace, and your life will flow with grace and ease. There is no greater reward!

14. Unique Soul Signature

You were born with seeds of brilliance and sparks of divine magnificence. Your essence is pure, beautiful, and divine, and not limited to your body.

You are encoded with all the tools to master this earthly realm, and your evolutionary potential is immense.

The process of discovery, revelation and remembrance drives a steady, progressive shift from ego-centered living to heart-centered living, bringing you back to your authentic self.

You have a unique soul signature.
Just like your handwritten signature has
a style and quality all its own,
so does your soul's.

Your soul has a vibrational essence, it's own signature reflecting the knowledge from your divinely designed soul lessons. Your soul signature is a uniquely divine expression in human form. Within you dwells infinite power, potential and possibility, waiting to be recognized. Simply being alive qualifies you to receive this eternal wisdom, so you may utilize its power to transform your life.

You are divinely unique and yet we are all ONE. We are made of one energy, one life-force, one consciousness. Still, every being on this planet is an individual expression of divine energy. *Your unique soul signature is a divinely inspired map to help navigate your life and understand the uniqueness of your soul's journey.* Embracing your soul signature provides the clarity and confidence you need to use *your gifts and talents to make the most of your journey.*

You entered this physical realm with a wide range of unique abilities. Some of these gifts may have been welcomed by your parents and community, and some may not have been appreciated as warmly as you would have liked. This is particularly true if you are strong in intuition, relationships, emotions, and creativity. These areas are not generally considered valuable by the analytical, left-brained, logically-oriented society which places a high value on analysis, data, and the physical world.

Now is the time to accept and cherish your unique gifts —despite any judgment from the external world. This is about honoring yourself and believing you have precious gifts to share. **It's time to re-value the energy of the sacred feminine, and blend this frequency with the masculine vibration that has dominated our world for so long.** One is not better than the other. The key is integrating both in our lives. It's time to realign and re-balance our world by merging intuition and creativity with the more traditional masculine energies in ways that generate greater awareness, harmony and unity.

Understanding your soul signature **is a process of accepting who you are, of gaining the keys to your personal sovereignty.** It is a process of remembrance which evolves as you move through your journey. Reclaim your personal sovereignty and discover your vast inner landscape. View your history and challenges from a broader perspective. Begin to heal and transform in ways which allow you to shine without inhibition or constraint.

Your Soul Signature is the foundation for a purposeful, harmonious, and balanced life. It is an energy, a vibration, frequency, color, and sound which reveal your unique experiences, talents, and abilities. Accept this and transform your experience. You will become the powerful and magnetic being you are intended to be. You are worthy and deserve greatness.

Never lose sight of your innate value
as a spiritual being temporarily housed in this physical body.

So, what are some other benefits of understanding your unique soul signature?

You will:

- Gain awareness of your true self
- Align your humanity with your divinity.
- Connect with infinite wisdom
- Understand your purpose
- Awaken your brilliance
- Deepen your connection to all beings
- Understand your divine blueprint
- Live more authentically
- Develop greater compassion
- Appreciate your unique talents
- Unleash hidden or suppressed attributes of your true self
- Rise above limiting patterns, perspectives and beliefs
- Avoid the limitations of energy density
- Consciously create your life
- Achieve self-acceptance
- Embrace every facet of yourself
- Feel liberated from past constraints
- Remember you are NOT your past, your fears, or your failures
- Realize your innate potential
- Connect to your highest vibrational frequency
- Tap into the knowledge you chose to bring to this lifetime
- Understand you are never separate from the divine.
- Realize everything you need already exists within you

⅄ Embrace your unique contribution to the world

⅄ Live with a renewed sense of passion and drive

⅄ Cease identifying with your ego and lead from your soul

With all these benefits, it's time to take some action!

It's application time again!

Please take out your notebooks and title this exercise:

Understanding my Soul Signature.

The goal of this exercise is to reveal your soul signature.

Ask yourself the following questions :

⅄ **"In what limiting ways have I defined myself and my life? What is my bigger story – the one my soul intends for me?" (Trust what comes through.)**

⅄ **"Since I chose to come here with lessons to learn, which repeated challenges highlight those primary lessons?**

⅄ **"What are my deepest wounds which require healing and attention?"**

⅄ **"Who have I not forgiven? Is it time to forgive myself for past choices?"**

⅄ **"Which gifts and abilities come most naturally to me? Am I sharing them?"**

⅄ **"If money were not a factor, what would I do each day to bring myself the greatest joy and satisfaction?**

⅄ **"In which unique ways can I express and reveal my true self, ways I can reconcile with my divine destiny?"**

⅄ **"Which action can I take to tap into the wellspring of my spiritual gifts and contribute to my own expansion?"**

Dedicate time and attention to expressing your divine essence to heal the wounds of yesterday, and the universe will respond in kind. A portal will open and you will be divinely guided by new inspiration and awareness. **You will become a natural magnet for the people, experiences, opportunities and adventures which** will propel you into the greatest expression of yourself.

Wondering what revealing your soul signature feels like?
Let's take a short journey together.

Imagine feeling completely connected, in tune and *in love* with everything in life. Imagine feeling so much compassion, forgiveness, understanding, connection and empathy that you actually shift from feeling it to "being it!" Imagine how it feels to be emotionally and mentally grounded with crystal clarity about who you are. Imagine feeling radiant and vibrant in every cell of your body. Imagine experiencing a sense of joy and enthusiasm in all you do each day, *recognizing* your purpose and feeling fulfilled as you live for that purpose.

Imagine how it feels to embrace your brilliance, to release all fear, worry and judgment and simply BE immersed in love. This is how it feels to be awakened to the purity and bliss of your true essence. Radiating your essence is as simple as choosing to do so. Step into your power and cultivate this connection to the "expansive you." Become aware of your magnificent light. It's time to journey into the infinite "you" to reveal your soul signature. Radiate your essence. This is who you are! It's time to share your magnificence with the world. The **worlds needs you, and you were meant to shine.**

15. FEMININE AND MASCULINE ENERGIES

We each have a dynamic mix of masculine and feminine energies. Masculine energies are characterized by linearity, goal-orientation, and mental focus. Feminine energies are circular, rooted in feeling and emotion, and are heart-centered. These energies are not mutually exclusive, so *they can be integrated in ways that expand our life experiences.*

Do you:

- get easily irritated
- get highly sensitive and often get your feelings hurt?
- react quickly and aggressively?
- need time alone or need to withdraw?
- experience bouts of insecurity and vulnerability?
- suffer from pain and anxiety?
- think others consider you rigid and fixed?

These feelings occur when your feminine and masculine energies are out of balance. When they are realigned, you feel whole and creative. **Your cognitive mind aligns with your heart, and you express yourself openly.** Life becomes a dance instead of a struggle. You create balance through awareness and the conscious integration of both energies within you.

Benefits from Creating Masculine/Feminine Balance:

You will remain centered, grounded and balanced in your daily life.

You will more easily connect with others.
You will express yourself more fully.
You will cope with your relationships and environment more harmoniously.
You will realize your potential and feel more fulfilled.
You will be more flexible and tolerant.
You will make balanced choices.

Our lives are polarized like a battery. There are many different ways to categorize the two charges, like yin and yang, but think of the masculine/feminine duality as the battery powering our universe. Like any battery, one end is negative, and one end is positive, neither of which is good or bad; both poles work together to run the flashlight. Each of us has varying degrees of masculine and feminine energy, so familiarize yourself with these two charges.

> *With awareness, you will blend your masculine and the feminine qualities to create the ultimate balance of a spiritual being living in a physical world.*

To realize your full potential, you must unify these energies before using them to accomplish your dreams. Blending the two energies will support your growth because each needs the other to become whole. ***To consciously evolve, you must transcend the duality of male and female energies. We are ageless, boundless, spiritual beings. But, while in physical form, we must balance the energies of yin and yang to achieve harmony.***

People who choose to embrace both their feminine and masculine energies become strong, wise, loving, creative, and empowered human beings. They appreciate the yang energy of taking action, while honoring the nurturing yin energy of stillness and gentleness.

It's application time again!

Please take out your notebooks. To begin the process of balancing your feminine and masculine energies, try the following exercises.

Title the first exercise: Releasing Masculine and Feminine Judgments

Whether you are a man or a woman, you may harbor hidden resentments about the opposite sex.

To unearth old, limiting beliefs, try the following awareness exercise.

Draw a line down the middle of the page.

At the top left please write "Women are..."
At the top right please write, "Men are ..."

Complete one side at a time without thinking too deeply about it. Don't screen or edit, just write until there's nothing left to say. You will probably end up with a combination of positive, negative, and neutral statements.

Review and reflect on what you've written and examine any emotions attached to your thoughts. Where do the positive and negative judgments come from? Are they long-standing? Did they begin in childhood?

Now complete the other side of the sheet.
Reflect on your judgments and emotions, trying to work out where in life they started.

Concentrate on your emotions and be honest about stereotyping men and women. Remember, your judgments of others are quite often judgments of yourself. *If you see men or women in a negative light, you won't be able to balance the two energies within you.*

Are you subconsciously suppressing your feminine or masculine energies?

Do you amplify one at the expense of the other?

These are difficult questions to answer, so please take all the time necessary to form an honest self-assessment.

The next step is to consciously *balance* these energies within you.

Balancing Your Masculine and Feminine Energies

Healthy role models are the best way to neutralize long-held prejudices about men and women. These may be in your life right now: sports and media stars, family members, or even historical figures. There are plenty to choose from.

To balance your feminine and masculine energies, actively promote the qualities of your role models, and tone down the actions and beliefs they would find abrasive or offensive. For example, if you tend to be over active, always on the go, doing, doing, doing, you most likely have a lot of masculine yang energy. To balance this, practice slowing down. Take time to meditate or pray each day. Go for slow nature walks or do a relaxing form of yoga. Quit using your analytical mind for a short time each day to experience the calming benefits of simply being, without any agenda or "to-do" list.

If you are nurturing, always agreeable and nice, satisfying everyone elses' needs but your own, you could use a dose of male, yang energy. Initiate a project just for yourself. Try warrior yoga poses. Set healthy, empowering boundaries by saying "No" at least once a week. Take inspired action each day.

Activate Your Yin and Yang Energy (Meditation Journey)

Here is an exercise to blend the flows of female and male energy, and bring them into balance. *Take this imagination journey with me.*

Sit with your eyes closed, consciously centered on your emotions. *Take a few deep breaths* (remember the power of 3) and allow your body to relax. *Use your intention to activate the flow of male yang energy.* Turn up the flame and feel it coursing through your body. It may help to visualize it first on the right side of your body and then spread it to the left side. Notice the quality of this energy. How would you describe it? As you sit with this energy, you will probably feel compelled to take action. Stay focused until the yang is completely activated.

Now activate the flow of your female yin energy. Open the faucet wide and feel its feminine power. Let it wash out the dominant male energy so you can tune into the pure vibration of the feminine. Notice the quality of this energy. How would you describe what you feel? Are there any "no" messages flowing through you, or do you feel yourself becoming more peaceful? Take your time. Stay with this energy until you feel complete.

Now, consciously and intentionally bring back the flow of masculine energy and allow it to blend with the feminine energy. How does it feel to have them balanced, merged, and acting in harmony? Do this exercise regularly. Some days you might notice you want more yin, while other days it would be appropriate to have more yang. Trust yourself to determine what you need in any given moment.

The next exercise to assist in further aligning your energy is a *CHAKRA MEDITATION*.

Integrate it into your self–nurturing routine.

Close your eyes and take three deep breaths. Visualize a beautiful golden white Light around your body, and feel yourself relax into that Light.

Focus on the base of your spine. Visualize a beautiful ball of red energy beginning to spin slowly. Take your time. You are activating your first chakra.

Now, focus your attention about three inches below your navel, visualizing a beautiful ball of orange energy there. Allow that ball of energy to spin slowly. Take your time. You are activating your second chakra.

Then, turn your attention to your solar plexus, visualizing a beautiful ball of yellow energy. Allow that ball of energy to spin slowly, as you activate your third chakra.

Next, focus on your heart, visualizing a beautiful ball of green energy. Allow that ball of energy to spin slowly as well. You are activating your fourth chakra.

Then, turn your attention to your throat, as you visualize a beautiful ball of blue energy. Set this ball of energy spinning with the others. Take your time. You are activating your fifth chakra.

Next, focus on the third eye between your brows and visualize a beautiful ball of indigo energy. As this ball of energy begins spinning, you are activating your sixth chakra.

Finally, turn your attention to the top of your head, visualizing a beautiful ball of violet energy. Set this ball of energy into a slow spin to activate your crown (7th) chakra.

Now, imagine you have walked down a long hallway toward a closed door. Put your hand on the door handle, open the door, and walk confidently inside. Find yourself in a large room with a beautiful, large, ornate mirror in the center. ***Stand directly in front of the mirror and see the reflection. Now for the exercise.***

Begin to consciously allow your masculine energy to change the reflection. *If you are female, see yourself as male. If you are male, see yourself as even more masculine than you feel in daily life.* Change this reflection into an image of masculinity down to the minutest detail possible. All the while, remember this is you, your masculine self. Look at this image until you feel comfortable with it.

Now, reach your hand into the mirror and *take the hand of your masculine image.* Pull this masculine self out of the mirror so he stands in front of you. Imagine a beam of green energy connecting your two hearts. Take him into a warm embrace until you *feel the boundaries between you lessening.* Feel your energies blending together until you are simply embracing yourself.

Now retrace your steps back into the hallway and close the door. Next to that door is a door into another room. Open it, walk inside, and see another large, ornate mirror. Walk up to the mirror and look at your usual reflection. *This time, consciously change your reflection into one of feminine energy.* If you are a woman, make the reflection even more feminine. If you are male, make the reflection your female counterpart. Take as much time as you need to become familiar with this feminine self.

Now, reach into the mirror and *take the hand of your feminine image,* pulling her out from the mirror until she is standing in front of you. Imagine another beam of green energy connecting your hearts. *Embrace this feminine image until you feel the boundaries between lessening and finally disappearing.* You have become one, and you stand embracing yourself.

Walk out of the room the way you came, closing the door behind you. Feel your consciousness re-inhabit the physical room. Feel your body return to the physical universe. When you feel ready, open your eyes.

This meditation is intended to first activate and then merge your feminine and masculine energies. It is a very empowering activity that grounds and centers you, so you can realize the fullness of your divine potential. Let this meditation fill you with light, love, and the acceptance of your ***perfectly balanced internal power. This power is your birthright.*** Embrace it. Acknowledge it. Know it. Feel it. Be it. It is YOU.

16. Evolving by Choice

We have an enormous capacity for growth, expansion, and love. We can allow the beauty of our infinite natures to shine, and **become trailblazing pioneers whose consciousness evolves by choice rather than chance.**

Our choices determine our reality.
We are not victims of circumstance.

Once we stop reacting to the world around us and begin to create our lives deliberately, one conscious choice after another, we allow the expansion promised by our birthright.

The conscious decision to evolve with awareness produces empowered souls ready to claim their creative power. We become ambassadors of expansion and love! We become love-finders instead of fault-finders, **and focus on what we want instead of what we don't want!** We must focus our attention on our abilities instead of our shortcomings.

Fighting against what we don't want perpetuates a negative cycle of disharmony and separation! Resisting anything keeps it firmly embedded in our energy fields. Evolving consciously means placing our full attention on promoting what we love instead of resisting what we fear. This supports the evolution of our world. There is no better gift to give or receive.

Love is the antidote to fear and it leads to purposeful evolution. This is precisely why we came to this planet! Choose cooperation over competition. This is the solution for loneliness and isolation. Evolve into the master you were intended to be! Open your heart and see the beauty in yourself and others. Revel in the empowerment of accepting others rather than judging them and creating separation.

By choosing to be an active participant in your own evolution, you will contribute to the collective evolutionary process. This is why you are alive at this time. If you are reading this book, you are intended to be a pioneer of expansion, a divinely designed agent of change.

You become your own catalyst for change by embracing each moment, so choose your path carefully. *Each choice is an expression of your personal power as your eternal soul directs you to* the "inner path" of self observation, self transcendence, and self-mastery. You must avoid leading from the external path which is littered with rigid opinions, criticism, and judgments.

> *Every choice you make is a sacred prayer, a powerful*
> *request to the universe to shape your reality.*

So be aware of what you pray for. There are no limits to what you can create, attract, or experience because every choice you make affects your energetic frequency. The resulting frequency determines your next set of choices. Choices open and close many doors, so be aware of *the impact YOUR choices have on your life.* We are made of energy and can choose the frequencies at which our emotions vibrate, so be aware of the emotional impact of your choices.

> *Emotions can vibrate at high or low frequencies.*
> *Fear, anger, guilt, shame, defeat, and*
> *worry are low vibrational energy.*
> *Choices made when guided by these emotions*
> *will keep you stuck in cycles of frustration.*

But, *the energies of love, peace, joy, enlightenment, and fun vibrate at much higher frequencies.* These emotions will positively impact your outer experiences, enlivening your reality with their high frequency vibrations.

Most personal challenges are caused by lower frequency emotional reactions. These reactions are often unconscious choices, so our goal is to make them conscious. Unconscious, repetitive reactions are difficult to manage because we lack awareness. Without self awareness, our responses remain rooted in low frequency cycles of negative emotion, holding back the joyful creation of the life you so richly deserve.

People speak about instincts and intuition as if they are one and the same. However, they are not the same at all. *Instinct* is governed by subconscious reactions that lead to certain repetitive behaviors. *Intuition, on the other hand stems from a conscious response.*

Instinct is reactive : Intuition is not.

Choices made instinctively keep you locked in restrictive cycles that can drive you (and those around you) crazy. *When you consciously make soul-driven choices, you will naturally have high vibrational emotions.*

> *By responding instead of reacting, you move
> beyond the old restrictive patterns.*

Don't underestimate the strength of these reactionary patterns; they can be so deeply ingrained that we don't realize we're stuck. To free ourselves from these cycles of discontent, we must consciously respond in empowering ways.

Our planet is a place which our souls deliberately chose to experience to further our expansion. By remembering this we become conscious creators of our experiences. We choose to experience our souls' potential and expression through positive, loving interactions OR though negative, fearful interactions. We choose freedom or limitation, they don't choose us. We clarify our preferences through contrasting experiences. Therefore, all experiences are valuable. The key is realizing our ability to gain clarity quickly instead of remaining stuck in our challenges.

Learning harmoniously doesn't eliminate all of our challenges. It simply provides the key to move through them with more grace and ease. Many challenging relationships are rooted in soul contracts we made with certain other souls prior to incarnating in this lifetime. *These soul contracts are divinely designed catalysts for our greatest learning lessons.* Our most challenging experiences offer the greatest opportunity for expansion. They can be viewed as gifts providing clarity for what we want and don't want.

If there is someone in your life repeatedly pushing your buttons, stop and ask yourself: "What is the deeper lesson here? What am I intended to learn? Is this THEIR lesson or mine?"

Sometimes the lesson is for both people, but not always. *Resisting our expansion by battling our challenges creates disharmony and dis-ease.* So, if you're stuck in situations where your buttons are continually being pushed, ask yourself if it's something you want to continue experiencing.

You have free will. You are the creative director of your life, so what do you want to experience? If you've had enough of an old, limiting pattern, look at it through the lens of your soul's growth, and re-direct your energy by reorienting your focus. Release what no longer benefits you. Integrate a higher level of understanding into your being by learning the lessons and moving on. *Remember, you choose the length, depth and severity of your lessons. If you re-attract a similar interaction in the future, use your wisdom to handle it differently.* This is conscious evolution. Remain aligned with the power and awareness of your soul, regardless of what is happening around you. Then, you will no longer attract the same challenges. You will move on to new ones, in a more advanced state of growth and expansion!

The keys to evolving by choice are discernment, introspection and self-honesty. You need these keys to navigate through the inevitable challenges, and to clearly interpret the lessons from these experiences.

> Make conscious CHOICES to create change instead
> of waiting for the world to change FOR you!

Being "At Choice" means you have discovered you are the writer, script editor and director of your experience. Many live "at effect" – blaming others, reacting to what others do, feeling imposed upon, fearing a lack of control, feeling victimized or powerless, resentful, or upset. You transform your world when you realize you have the power to be the CHOOSER, and to be "At Choice" in your life.

We are each sovereign beings with free will. There is no single right answer or single way to choose. An infinite number of outcomes can emerge depending on the energy we choose to focus on in each situation. *We change outcomes and experiences by changing our perspective, by simply shifting our focus. We choose which reality to create.* We choose to evolve beyond limiting factors which deny our infinitely creative and powerful nature. We must embrace our power to choose the frequencies which create the realities we wish to experience.

There is no wrong way to achieve mastery of yourself. Guide yourself from within. *Your heart is the gateway to expansive consciousness.* Your source identity dwells there, so let your heart guide your choices. ur truths. Upgrade your entire life experience by following your heart's advice.

Self limiting or self destructive patterns of behavior result from choices which are not aligned with your true self. You must realize your

moment-to- moment ability to choose, to reclaim your creative power. Break free! Become aware of self–destructive patterns. Pause, and choose again. It can be that simple. A wide range of new options is always available, you've just forgotten them. You have the power to choose, and your choices will determine the quality, depth, and expansiveness of your experience.

Changes in your external world must occur within you first.

You choose to open the door, to allow something new and different into your life. This is where the magic happens. When you take hold of the steering wheel and actively turn in the direction of your choice, "miracles" become the norm. **Embrace your power to choose infinite wealth, health, joy, opportunity, peace and bliss beyond measure!** This is your choice every moment of your life.

Activating your power of choice is something you do on a daily basis. Use your creative power as often as possible. Begin each day with the intention to connect with your higher self and your spiritual support team. We all have one! This can include your higher self, angels, guides, archangels, ascended masters, or the celestial hierarchy. This intentional opening to divine insight will set the stage for the conscious creation of your day.

Once you've decided to connect with your divine "helpers", ask yourself the following questions:

ᐱ "Which opportunities for love, connection, joy and wealth do I want today? What would it take for me to notice and seize these opportunities?"

ᐱ "Which choices will allow me to expand my perspective, my gifts, my relationships, my business and my health?"

⚔ "What divine information, inspiration, or guidance would support my soul's evolution today?

Ask, then open yourself to the answers. They may come instantly, so write them down without analyzing or judging. The answers may come via synchronicity during your day. Trust you will receive the proper guidance. Expect it. Then, simply remain open to the divine signs pointing you toward your answers and opportunities.

Conscious evolution requires divine guidance. Be conscious of what you ask for, and ask in an affirmative way. If you are sick, don't ask for help with your symptoms. ***Instead, ask for divine help to return to "radiant, perfect health and balance."*** If you want to drop a few pounds, don't ask to lose the weight. Ask to "release" any extra weight in the "highest and best way possible." If you ask for strength to build a character trait like "more patience," expect "lessons" in patience, because that is the best way to learn and master your energy. You will be sent the experiences you need to learn patience. Start by affirming "I Am Patient," because stating "I Am Patient" activates the energy of patience within you.

If you are not sure what to ask for, ***simply ask for divine awareness so you can respond to your life in the most empowering way possible.*** A grander lens and a broader perspective can shift your experience instantly and positively.

The key to evolving by choice rather than chance is awareness of your power to choose. Activate it, then use it to create the life you deserve. When you ask questions like the ones listed above, you connect with your higher self. Then, simply pay attention! Notice the subtle signs and inner nudges. ***Life will no longer happen TO YOU after you become a powerful, conscious creator, and decision maker.*** You will hear, trust, and follow your internal GPS. You will no longer tolerate, accept, or BE anything less than your own source of power and creation. Empowering? It's your option at all times.

IT'S APPLICATION TIME AGAIN!

Please take out your notebooks and title this exercise:

"What am I consistently choosing?"

Ask yourself that question and allow your responses to come through naturally. Trust what comes through. This will bring to the surface old patterns which need to be released. *What have you been choosing most consistently for yourself – perhaps for years – that might be keeping you stuck?* Embrace your creative power and choose again.

Get honest with yourself as you create this list. Give yourself full permission to choose again! You have the power to choose. Clear the old negative energy and open yourself to inspiration from the divine.

Realize how powerful you are as a choice maker!

Now is the time to upgrade from the old finite menu of experiences to the infinite menu. Revel in infinite choice, possibility, and opportunity, and the universe will realign itself with your new higher frequency. Walls crumble and doors open.

Step into the realm of conscious evolution, where life occurs by choice, and not by chance.

17. THE BLUEPRINT OF YOUR DIVINE DESTINY

Before we arrive on this planet, we set intentions for what we wish to experience while focused in physical form. We create road-maps for our journeys. This happens with the divine assistance of our support teams in the non-physical realms. We compile these blueprints very carefully, including the soul lessons we wish to learn, ways to implement specific strengths and abilities, as well as desired new qualities to assist in the the spiritual evolution of our souls. Expansion in every form is written into each blueprint, to be worked out with new families and relationships. All family members, close friends, and many acquaintances are carefully selected during this pre-incarnation period.

Although we are destined to follow the plans outlined in our blueprints, we come into this world as sovereign beings.

We choose the difficulty and length of our upcoming challenges, and the manner in which we will move through the divinely designed experiences of our new lives.

Each lifetime is a step toward remembering our infinite natures, so our destiny blueprints are a collection of divinely inspired opportunities.

All the pre-planning allows us to achieve our greatest spiritual potential as physical beings on earth.

NOW is the time to rise above limits, to shed all toxic energies as we move back toward the light. *Expand beyond today's constraints to reach a state of detached, yet compassionate emotional mastery.*

How? With awareness, conscious effort and commitment. Begin by clearing out old, limiting patterns of behavior which keep you from remembering the purity of your eternal spirit. Optimize your life by tuning into the divine frequencies and focusing on anything that brings you joy. Old negative cycles can be released as we merge with the totality of potential at the core of our divine natures.

> *Your divine destiny is always unfolding.*
> **Your blueprint becomes the inner guidance system**
> **prompting you to make the best choices**
> **as you create your personal heaven on earth.**

Everyday, ask for divine assistance to remain centered on your path. Connect with your spiritual team of light each morning and affirm your desire to fulfill your divine destiny. Ask for clear details, then watch for signs and clues as your day progresses. Your emotions will indicate when you are on your path and when you've taken a unnecessary detour. Positive emotions reflect alignment with your blueprint. Negative emotion reflects resistance to it. It's that simple.

Are you ready to make the changes necessary to move forward in your expansion? Consciously set the intention and ask for support. Clear your body, mind and spirit of outdated energy patterns which block your path by shifting your focus. ***See with new eyes, feel with an open heart, and realize your divinely designed potential. That's why you're here.***

Connecting daily with your higher self and spiritual support team will give you the focus and confidence to overcome obstacles, and to release any doubts, fears, and confusion. Start each morning by saying: "I am aligned with my divine mission and I am moving forward. Everything is always working out for me." Then, ***ask your spiritual support team for a new set of options to bring you closer to the fulfillment of your soul's destiny***. Trust that as you set this intention, the road ahead will reveal itself with ease.

There is no need to force, push against or make things happen. In fact, that resistance only prevents you from noticing open doors. ***When you are in alignment, life flow easily.*** When you're not, walls appear everywhere.

We have so many miraculous new opportunities for growth, wellness and unconditional love. NOW is the time to experience Unity over Division and Connection over Separation. ***We do this with our focus. We do this by being pro-active instead of reactive.*** Our goal should be consistently placing our predominant attention on thoughts, words and actions that cause us to feel in sync with our divinity.

All souls share the same universal divinity, the eternal energy of God. ***We are all kindred spirits sharing unique earthly experiences intended to provide us with opportunities for expansion.*** We must all remember our divine heritage to emerge from limiting three dimensional "tunnels". These self-made tunnels block the light and prevent us from seeing the wonderful opportunities around us each day. We create our own tunnels, so we can choose to emerge from them by assuming a broader perspective and making new choices. We can end the ***tunnel-vision preventing us from remembering our true natures.***

Open the door to your innate wisdom and soul-memory. Don't underestimate the power of your mind and emotions to create this new perspective. Your burdens increase when focused upon. Your abundance also increases when focused upon.

You cannot be a catalyst for success while focused on fear.
You cannot be a catalyst for wellness while focused on illness.

You can create internal shifts this instant! Shift your focus and expectations, and you will generate a positive new vibrational signal. This paves the way for authentic joy and well being. Remember how powerful you truly are. ***Design your destiny by realizing the outer world reflects your consistently held thoughts and beliefs.*** If you consistently attract people who dis-empower you, you must examine your own energy and change its frequency. Alter your thoughts to change your reality. Imagine each day as an opportunity to experience a new reality reflecting your wholeness and potential. Claim your divine right to a clean slate.

As you increase your vibration, your external experiences will reflect the perfection of your divine blueprint. The inner creates the outer. By ***choosing to activate your inner light, you affect the consciousness of everyone you encounter, creating a ripple effect which enhances*** the consciousness of the entire planet. YES, you are that powerful.

You may wonder how to tell if you're on the "right" path, the one aligned with the blueprint of your destiny. A clear indicator of this is feeling "in sync". When you are on your divinely designed path, things fall into place easily. Your creativity flows effortlessly and your decisions feel divinely supported. ou feel inspired to take action. If you don't feel this, you must realign yourself with your divine blueprint by reminding yourself of your original mission. You must be willing to look at any imbalances or limiting patterns, and be very honest with yourself about your present situation. You can always get back on track.

It's application time again!

Please take out your notebooks and title this exercise:

Aligning My Path with my Divine Blueprint.

Create two columns.

Title the first one: Imbalances.

Under this column, write down reasons you don't feel 'in sync." These can be physical, emotional, mental, spiritual, professional, or romantic. Identify where and when you feel imbalanced. Your masculine and feminine energies might be imbalanced. This is important to address.

Title your second column Limiting Patterns.

Which patterns of thinking, speaking, reacting, believing and feeling might limit your day to day experiences? Do you think harshly about yourself? Do you speak unkindly about others? Do you believe you are worthy of love and joy? Do you react more than you respond? Do you believe the world is a safe, loving place? Do your thoughts reflect the reality you wish to create and experience?

Creating these lists will bring an immense clarity to you regain balance, confidence, passion and hope.

These lists will help you clearly identify distractions to be discarded and all the beauty you need to embrace. *Just ask, intend and then pay attention!* Your journey is guided by a divine support team who support your growth by lighting your path.

As you begin to vibrate on your original frequency, *your soul signature remembers how to express its purpose in the world*. Your powerful inner guidance system leads you to experiences that contribute to your expansion.

> *Each day is a an opportunity for your destiny*
> *to unfold with grace and ease.*
> *Enjoy bliss, ease, and harmony as you*
> *activate your divine blueprint.*

What could be better than that?

18. Destiny and Free Will

We talk of your soul's blueprint, but is your life predestined or does free will create your reality? *The two co-exist.*

*Certain moments, events, and individuals are destined
to enter your life because they are part of your divine blueprint.
But you also have free will,
which determines when you open or close
the doors for those people and events.*

Every choice you make closes one door and opens another. *Your soul is meant to fulfill a particular destiny in this lifetime, but the way you do so is up to you.* Your primary experiences are divinely designed in advance, but you control the timing of your spiritual chronicle. Either you pay attention to the signs along the way (that are meant to steer you in the direction best suited to your soul's growth and evolution) or you don't! You cannot control the lives of others, *but you do choose your own responses, attitudes, and actions*. Free will enables you to make wise choices aligned with your soul's blueprint, as long as you listen to your intuition, the ever-present voice within.

You know by now that before you are born, you work with your spiritual support team in the higher realms to plan your next incarnation. The resulting blueprint includes your career, life lessons, and the major life relationships like parents, siblings, romantic partners, and children. Life is a maze, from birth to death. *Along the twisting corridors of your personal maze, your higher self and spiritual support team place major life events in your path.* This is the predestined aspect of your life. The way you navigate each of these events is where your free will comes into play!

After birth, you forget what your upcoming maze looks like, but you are always intuitively guided and naturally attracted to the pre-destined events on your blueprint. *Intuition usually nudges you into the particular corridors leading to your soul's destiny,* but sometimes, you run into a dead end and must back track. In the end though, you emerge from this life a wiser soul.

> *What happens when something goes "wrong?"*
> *Actually, there are no "wrong" turns, just experiences.*

Free will is not predictable. Your higher self and spiritual guides get you to your life events, but *you freely decide you will go, how long it will take to get there, and who you choose to bring along.* To confuse matters, other people's mazes intersect yours (like your future spouse or child), making it more challenging to navigate your own path. These distractions may derail you at times, but *your angels, guides and higher self will intervene to help redirect you.* They will lead you to water, but you will drink it when you're thirsty. Pay attention, notice the divinely designed nudges from your spiritual support team in the form of intuitive flashes. If you don't make it to every pre-destined event on your blueprint, that's okay. Those events will reappear in a different lifetime.

While traveling through life, notice the signposts. Beware of long and hopeless corridors leading to frustration. Pay attention to reach all your divinely designed blueprint experiences with as much grace and ease as possible! *If you don't like where you're headed, change it!* You are the navigator. You decide the direction. You are never stuck on a dead end road unless you choose to be.

It's application time again!

Please take out your notebooks and title this exercise:

Living Consciously!

Develop an attitude of positive expectancy to design your own destiny effectively. This paves the way for a fulfilling life.

The following tips will help create a new daily habit for you.

First, vividly imagine your day. See with your soul's eyes. Create a concise and clear image of your expectations. Visualize your meetings and interactions going exceedingly well. There are no limits to your creative abilities! You will attract what you first create in your imagination.

Second, add emotion. Add deep emotion to your visualization. This is the spiritual fuel that brings your visualization to life. So, feel the connections and interactions as though they are already happening.

Third, believe. However vividly imagined and ardently desired, you must believe in your worthiness and ability to turn your intentions into reality. You must believe in your creative potential!

Fourth, enthusiastically take action. Enthusiasm and action are powerfully effective partners in bringing your visualizations into reality. Actions empowered by enthusiasm create the fertile soil to nurture success.

Even after applying this exercise daily, you won't be free from disappointment, frustration, or challenges. But you will be in the position to ***transform problems into opportunities and adversity into strengths.*** You will proactively create your day instead of reacting haphazardly.

Destiny is a straight line, while free will is a wave fluctuating above and below that line. ***You are never forced to live your destiny, but you are tethered to it.***

Your destiny is a progression of growth and development,
not a destination.
It is an unfolding spiritual chronicle,
shaped as you move along your path.

The more spiritually "awake" you become, the more clearly you see doors opening and closing on your journey. This accelerated awareness is directly influenced by your decisions. Life is much more rewarding when you grab the wheel and consciously steer it toward your highest potential. *Evaluating potential pathways while remaining clear about your choices will transform life from a mystery into a spiritual quest.*

Seek your deepest desires, follow your intuition, and heal yourself from the inside-out. Live your dreams by aligning your life with your soul's divine blueprint.

You are the only one responsible for creating your life story.
Do not allow it to be determined by the choices of others.
Mold, shape, and design your day-to-day reality any way you choose.
Recognizing this powerful truth is "liberation."

Feel gratitude every moment of the journey and *recognize your power to direct your unfolding spiritual chronicle.* You have far more creative power that you realize.

19. Being "Spiritual"

Defining spirituality is challenging in this modern, ever-changing world. Spiritual living is an essential component of fulfillment, but defining it often limits its meaning. The world is undergoing a powerful shift in consciousness, with more and more people labeling themselves "spiritual" or "religious."

We are on unique journeys of awakening, remembering our divine natures while still in this physical form, but no one path is better than another.

When we claim one route to God superior to another, we speak from ego and not spirit. Spirituality is not necessarily the same thing as religion, but both serve a purpose in our evolution as human beings. Religion can be a beautiful source of connection and guidance, giving us an elevated awareness of our integrity and morality. But *labeling people's beliefs and inclinations as "good/bad" or "right/ wrong"* is divisive and distracts us from the original purpose of religion.

While many religions have inflexible set of beliefs, spirituality is non judgmental and flexible. Religious dogmas often hide the truth of our divinity, with their rigid beliefs preventing us from recognizing the oneness of all living beings. The experience of "oneness" or "unity consciousness" is spiritual.

Seeing the divinity in all people, all religions, and all paths is liberating.

Teachings which increase our prejudices or narrow our beliefs will result in unnecessary guilt, and intolerance, preventing us from truly seeing the divine nature in ourselves and others. So, religions which foster fear or guilt prevent individuals from remembering the core teachings which should unite us as divine souls.

Where there is fear and judgment, we will not find the divine love, unity and peace which are essential parts of the discovery process for souls incarnated on our planet. All religious teachings share a beautiful, common thread which carries a universal truth. This truth is a shared vision which brings connection and a sense of oneness to people all over the world. Sadly, when each religion holds out its own scriptures as the only path to divinity, the truth is lost.

The world would be a much more harmonious place if ***humanity could recognize and accept the beauty in all paths, realizing that each springs from the same source.***

We needn't attend church to be spiritually aware and engaged with our divinity. ***Spirituality is internally rooted, a remembrance of our innate wholeness and divinity.*** Its expression is not limited to any particular set of beliefs. Spirituality is a feeling of unity, oneness, and connection with God, the divine creative force who binds us together. The Creator is felt and known through intimate sharing with others, through meditation, and communing with nature, or simply being of service.

Spiritual experiences expand the mind and awaken the heart and spirit. Remembering our true, divine nature brings us peace. ***When we love and accept, our spiritual natures glow on everyone around us.*** We feel and see the spiritual nature in others, and have no expectation or judgment because spirituality is rooted in divine love. No one can tell us what a spiritual experience "must be." Each path is unique, guided by each soul's blueprint for its journey through life. ***We come to live authentically when we nurture our unique spiritual selves.***

As we integrate spirit into form, we become "divine humans." We see beauty everywhere, and accept ourselves and others without judgment.

> *As "divine humans," we focus on what unites*
> *us rather than our differences.*

We learn the soul lessons we came here to learn, and the past falls away. Forgiveness, understanding and acceptance connect us with our divine nature, and our hearts come to see the divine beauty in others.

Internal and external suffering is a temporary disconnect from the memory of our divinity. We must have compassion for others and extend forgiveness to all.

> *We are on unique journeys, at different speeds,*
> *navigating our individual paths with differing levels of awareness.*

When we make peace with ourselves and others, we become content in our lives. We are spiritual beings exploring and expanding our divine nature in physical form. It is easy to get caught up in the drama of three dimensional living, but we always have the power to explore the deeper meaning behind our challenges.

> *The divine invitation to remember our true*
> *natures is encoded in our souls.*
> *It's up to each of us to accept this invitation.*

We choose the level of participation on our journeys. There is no right or wrong way to experience our humanity. All paths eventually lead home. So, we must take the best from religion, but eliminate any intolerance. The essence of spiritual awareness is understanding that God lives within us, not outside of us. *To understand our divine purpose, we must listen to and trust our internal guidance system.*

We cannot see the true light and divinity in our souls if we adhere to any rigid dogma.

Mutual respect and compassion are the ways we unite in harmony with our fellow man. This is how we become divinely human. May we all come to see and feel the truth, to remember who we truly are. May we all strive to see the beauty, light and divinity within ourselves and one another, with each doing his part to make this world a better place. Now is the time to make a difference. We do this by focusing on our light and coming into personal alignment with the totality of who we are. Our example will shine more brightly than words every could.

Our true nature is beyond measure because it is the pure knowledge of God. *We are infinite beings of unconditional love and creativity, experiencing and expressing our divinity through our physical bodies.* We are not, nor have we ever been, separated from the pure love and intelligence of "God."

"God" is quite simply the Divine Source emanating from the spiritual realms on an infinite range of frequencies. We all spring from this Divine Source and remain one with the Divine as beings of love, peace, harmony, and creative intelligence even as we exist in physical form. We are Divine Light are our core. We become specifically and temporarily focused in this physical realm as humans while simultaneously existing in the non-physical realms.

We are never separate from God,
we are eternally connected to the divine,
one another, and all that exists.

It's application time!

Please take out your notebooks and title this exercise:

"Embracing the Divinity Within."

Please create two lists.

The first list will include all the reasons you believe you are separate from God, reasons like lack of worthiness or fear.

Your second list will include all the reasons you feel separate from others. The purpose in creating these lists is to **highlight any beliefs which prevent you from accepting your divine nature.**

The final part of the exercise will be to make a list of all the aspects of "oneness." For example, unconditional love, forgiveness, tolerance or global harmony could be on your list. There is no right or wrong way to do this. Once you've completed all of your lists, ask yourself which list is better aligned with your soul. Explore your beliefs and decide which ones you are ready to let go of, and which you wish to expand on to find greater peace with others and greater connection with your divine nature.

Spiritual awareness involves remembering your divine nature. While religion often feels like an obligation, true spiritual connection brings a sense of contentment to the roots of your soul. There are many aspects of truth. There is no "right" or "wrong" except that which we label as much. Choose those which feel best for you and find the joy in YOUR journey.

PART III
Soul-Driven Success

20. SOUL DRIVEN GOALS

What are the ingredients of a soulfully rewarding journey? Happiness, spontaneity, humor, flexibility, appreciation and contentment! Inspired goals support the unfolding of your soul-driven journey, so it's helpful to have steps to achieve these goals.

First, *let's redefine goal-setting.*

> *As you focus on less linear strategies, you allow for greater fluidity and fun!*

My intention is to support you in integrating tools that naturally support the unfolding of your divine destiny with grace and ease. You will feel lighter when you abandon ego-driven goals for soul-inspired goals. This will allow you to experience greater harmony as your destiny unfolds.

These short and simple ten steps will <u>jump-start the creative process!</u>

1. **Know what you want and understand what's preventing you from realizing the dreams of your body/mind/spirit.**

Be clear about what you want. Focus on your soul's deepest desires and dreams, and release the mental, emotional, physical and spiritual roadblocks that prevent you from having what you want!

2. Commit to creating positive change.

Commitment is key! Your level of commitment TO YOUR OWN HAPPINESS determines success (moving forward) or failure (stagnancy or moving backward.) Commitment is the foundation for your success. A consistently held intention to be the source of your own happiness will naturally and effortlessly attract the opportunities for you to realize your dreams. Choose the accelerated path!

3. Become aware of old, limiting patterns!

Recognize patterns of thought, emotion and behavior that stem from old, limiting beliefs. This will bring you one step closer to experiencing true personal empowerment and liberation. Be aware of the words and expectations that imprison you in a negative mind set. Commit to celebrating your day-to-day and moment-to-moment ability to rise above the limits of yesterday!

4. Create new empowering habits to replace old limiting ones.

This step is crucial! Choose to imprint positive new thoughts, words, and behavior patterns on your consciousness. Allow these attributes to attract positive experiences, people and opportunities. See the world around you with new eyes, and new doors of opportunity will appear to replace the old walls of restriction!

5. Integrate new habits into your life with enthusiasm and positive expectation.

Take inspired action to implement new empowering habits, paving the way for phenomenal results in your life. These internal shifts will expand and enhance your experiences in life. New positive patterns will increase your energy in ways that keep you constantly positioned to realize your dreams.

6. Visualize your ideal future.

Visualization is a key component in the process of bringing your dreams to life. When you clearly visualize your ideal future as if it already your personal reality, you become a magnet for the information, inspiration, people and opportunities that will carry you to your goals. You will understand just how powerful you truly are.

7. Create AND ALLOW for a healthy, supportive environment and positive relationships.

The process of "allowing" must be chosen on a daily basis. (You cannot resist and receive at the same time!) Make conscious choices, set clear and positive expectations, and allow for success-full, nurturing relationships and joyful experiences to permeate your daily life. Consciously create an environment where you can THRIVE. Shift from surviving to thriving. It makes the ride so much more fun!

8. Seize new opportunities for success.

Pay attention to new circumstances and individuals crossing your path. Acknowledge these opportunities and take action to realize your goals. Don't hesitate to respond! Be grateful for these divinely designed opportunities, and remember they have been delivered to you as part of your soul's blueprint.

9. Believe you are worthy.

Believe you are a beautiful, radiant soul worthy of phenomenal success and prosperity. Regardless of your past, you choose your future. Exercise your innate power to attract all the people and opportunities required to reach your goals. It is inside you, and no one on the outside can give it to you.

10. Live with an attitude of gratitude.

A consistently chosen "attitude of gratitude" is a divinely magnetic state of mind which attracts even greater abundance and blessings. See your dreams come alive before your eyes and give sincere thanks for them.

Believe you are worthy of these gifts, capable of receiving even greater success, and stay receptive to limitless abundance!

21. FLEXIBILITY

We stretch our physical muscles, so why not stretch our mental, emotional and spiritual muscles as well? *We need flexibility in ALL aspects of life*, because life is filled with unexpected twists and turns.

Either we bend, or we get stuck, physically AND spiritually!

Consciously moving toward our challenges instead of back-pedaling away from them keeps us in the flow. This is where the magic happens.

- *How receptive are YOU to change?*
- *How responsive are YOU to new ideas?*
- *Do your beliefs separate you from others?*

A surefire way to experience loneliness is to believe your way is the only way, and insisting others agree with you. *Forcing your position on others causes immediate disconnection*, and is an absolute waste of energy!

Feeling threatened or angry when your beliefs are questioned means you value being right over being happy. Living inflexibly, always on the defensive, is simply no fun! And, it's certainly no fun for the people around you! *Insisting on having your own way sets you on the fast-track to unhappiness.* Rigid thoughts or beliefs lead to power struggles and ultimately to separation. Insisting on "shoulds" and "musts" leads directly to endless disappointment and disconnection.

How does this affect relationships? Life is a web of systems, of patterns of behavior governing how two or more individuals interact.

A couple, family, neighborhood and even our planet are all examples of systems. Systems cover the entire gamut, from completely open to completely closed. In open systems, people exchange ideas and accept feedback, allowing everyone to grow and evolve. A closed system blocks new input, preventing change and protecting the status quo. The feedback loop simply recycles the same information. Our goal should always be to live openly!

Anyone who needs to be right all of the time is a closed system, unwilling to accept challenges to their beliefs and ideas. Closed people are often tense, angry, and bitter. Could this be YOU? If so, expect others to keep their distance, reinforcing your closed system and cutting you off from the experiences of intimacy and connection.

People become closed because their egos create defenses to preserve a sense of well-being. Blaming others becomes a defense mechanism, but projecting the problem outside one's self only reinforces the sense of self righteousness. Inner tension is not eased because the ego knows something is wrong.

We all have moments when we feel the need to be right, to have our own way. But happiness stems from connection! ***Connections form when we find common ground*** and acknowledge each others' worthiness. Relinquish the need to control, and find that harmony feels much better than friction!

Please examine yourself for any rigid characteristics that might impede YOUR growth and expansion. (Be sure to put on your self-compassion hat while doing this exercise!)

Examples of rigidity (lack of flexibility) include:

- ⚔ An insatiable need to be right (which masks a deep fear of being wrong.)
- ⚔ A tendency to expect others to "see it your way."

⅄ An inability to say, "I don't know," or "I was wrong."

⅄ Feeling threatened when new ideas come from others.

⅄ Fear new information that unsettles existing beliefs.

⅄ Fear of letting go, of not being in control of self at all times.

⅄ Preoccupation with the approval of others.

⅄ The need to be seen as tough, powerful and strong.

⅄ Pride in always being rational and logical.

⅄ Being uncomfortable expressing emotions or sensitive feelings.

⅄ Experiencing shame and fear when feeling vulnerable or insecure.

⅄ Severe discomfort about having bad feelings.

⅄ A strong belief that those who disagree with you are wrong.

⅄ A tendency to use anger, withdrawal or blame to settle arguments.

Ask yourself: *"Do I want to be right or do I want to be happy?"*

The conscious choice to tear down your walls will lead to the intimacy and connection you desire and deserve. As you become more open, you develop greater self trust and understanding, which makes it far easier to take responsibility for your part in conflict. Conflict becomes an opportunity for growth each time you face the fear of being wrong and work through it. Inflexibility fosters predictability, fooling us into feeling "safe" because it keeps anxiety at bay. But *with greater openness and flexibility, life becomes much more exciting. Choices, alternatives and adventures multiply!*

Release your need to control others, and find how much more energy you have for things that actually matter. Being in charge of everything is a heavy, time-consuming job! You actually become more powerful when you learn to share the power.

Deep down, what we most desire is to be loved.
We want to feel safe, to be heard and understood.

The fear of losing control is a sign we need love but don't know how to get it. Anger at challenges is a masked cry for love. Pull down the walls of separation, build connections through flexibility, communication, and conflict resolution. Commit to being an open person and move that much closer to true soul fulfillment.

How does this happen? ***The need to be right can be overcome if you are honest with yourself about being adamant or inflexible.*** Overcoming rigid patterns will increase your personal power. Instead of having power over others, you develop power over yourself. This is true self-esteem!

- **Do you want to be right or do you want to be happy?**
- **Do you want to get your own way or do you want to feel connected to others?**
- **Are you willing to balance your logical left brain with your intuitive right brain to become a well-rounded person?**

Open your heart, mind and spirit to new concepts and fresh ideas and begin vibrant living! ***Be progressive instead of regressive.*** Resisting change multiplies the levels of stress and increases the problems in your path. Remain flexible (even in the midst of significant change or chaos)to achieve your full potential. Doors will open, and opportunities appear because you will be at peace with yourself.

Too narrow a focus diminishes your creative potential. Without flexibility, you will not see solutions to conflict, nor will you get the love and support you need in life. ***Divine guidance toward practical solutions comes when your mind and heart are open, and your spirit is leading the way***. See even the most challenging people and situations through the eyes of love and compassion and those challenges will become rewards. Flexibility leads to a sense of understanding and harmony, and leaves you grounded through the most trying times.

People who are emotionally, mentally, and spiritually flexible:

⅄ Possess an unstoppable attitude.

⅄ Feel content with life.

⅄ Don't sweat the small stuff.

⅄ Embrace adventure.

⅄ Have a zest for living.

⅄ Laugh often and have fun each day.

⅄ Deal with stress more easily and bounce back quickly from adversity.

⅄ Live with meaning and purpose, both personally and professionally.

⅄ Eagerly learn new lessons.

⅄ Adapt gracefully to life's twists and turns.

⅄ Welcome positive change.

⅄ Know the importance of balance between work and play, rest and activity.

⅄ Build and maintain fulfilling relationships.

⅄ Are fueled by a positive attitude, self-confidence and high self-esteem.

We all suffer disappointments and losses that cause sadness, anxiety, and stress. **Open and flexible people have a natural ability to bounce back more easily and quickly from adversity, trauma, and stress.** Flexible souls are resilient, equipped with the right tools to cope with difficult situations while maintaining a positive outlook. They remain adaptable and creative in bad times as well as good.

> *Flexibility means bending but not breaking,*
> *adapting without losing the essence of yourself.*

Know the general direction, but accept and enjoy the detours. Flexibility means changing course when opportunities to learn and grow appear. See challenges as learning tools, opportunities to become stronger, wiser versions of ourselves. Most importantly, flexibility *is preparing for and embracing change instead of fearing it.*

The more flexible and balanced you are, the less likely you are to over-react to situations in your life. This means being open-minded and fluid, not stiff necked and obstinate. The cure for the latter? **Listen. Remain grounded. Be open. Allow growth.** The alternative is to be stubborn, closed-minded and imbalanced, consistently fueling conflict. Which sounds better? Why not choose flexibility and lead by example? *Integrate spiritual stretching into your daily routine!*

It's application time!

Please take out your notebooks and title this exercise:

Spiritual Stretching: My Flexibility Checklist.

Read the questions and write any insights you have gained. The goal is to empower yourself to focus on *creating new, more fulfilling experiences by adopting a more flexible attitude and outlook:*

- **Is my body tense?** Tension mirrors a rigid belief, outlook or behavior pattern. Breathe deeply, be compassionate with yourself, and journal your answers. Which aspects of your life need more flexibility?
- **Do I have any unbending rules in your life and relationships?** If so, what are they? Are they creating the life and relationships you desire? Challenge yourself to notice these rigidities. Would it help to dump these rules and go with the flow instead?
- **Am I open to making behavioral adjustments to learn and grow?** Contemplate the cost of remaining resistant and inflexible. Think of the limits you place on your growth.
- **Am I defined by certain moods?** If so, respond in a different way. Detach yourself from the heaviness of these moods and choose an alternative emotional state such as compassion.

↟ ***Am I agenda driven?*** Do I feel the need to persuade others to believe as I do, regardless of the stress I create between myself and others?

↟ ***Am I willing to embrace new experiences and ideas outside my psychological and cultural comfort zones?*** If not, challenge yourself to expand! No one can keep you in a box but you.

↟ ***Am I a creature of habit, finding it hard to shift my rigid expectations?*** If so, choose new and different ways of doing things to liberate yourself and those around you. Go with the flow a little more.

Unconscious patterns of rigid behavior stand in the way of our happiness! Bring them to the surface, and discard them! Inflexibility fuels frustration with ourselves and others. It creates tension and stress in our relationships. ***The pressure of struggling to new situations can be wake up calls.*** These moments are invitations to stretch beyond our comfort zones and expand our hearts, minds and spirits to allow for grace and harmony.

> *Every challenging person and situation is a teacher,*
> *offering divinely designed opportunities*
> *for growth, understanding, compassion, and healing.*

When we approach life in this manner, without resisting these circumstances and individuals, life takes on a broader, more expansive meaning. ***When we view our challenges as beautiful hidden jewels , we become all the wealthier.***

Stretch your mental, emotional and spiritual muscles today and notice how laughter, joy, and love flow into your life with greater ease. Your inspired ways will generate a delightful ripple effect. This is the greatest gift you can give yourself or your loved ones.

22. EMPOWERING VOCABULARY

The spoken word has tremendous power. The way we describe the present determines the way our tomorrows unfold!

Your word is your wand, filled with magical power!

- ⋏ What is the very first thing you say to yourself when you wake up in the morning?
- ⋏ The first words to your loved ones?
- ⋏ The last thought you communicate before you go to sleep at night?

You can mold your surroundings by choosing your words to generate a powerful new vocabulary which reflects the life of your dreams. *Health replaces sickness, abundance replaces lack, and joy replaces sorrow.*

By expanding your vocabulary, you change your entire life.

The secret? Certain empowering words will transform your life, giving you *the power to experience more success than you ever thought possible!*

What kind of future is your current vocabulary creating? How empowering are the words you speak today? Do they propel you forward into greater health, wealth, joy, and success, or do they create obstacles to the abundance and love you deserve? Do your words enhance the quality of your life or diminish it?

Words bring our intentions to life by transmitting certain vibrations. *Words lift us up or drag us down, and either attract or repel opportunities.* Importantly, they will always fill us with absolute joy, enthusiasm and inspiration if used positively and effectively. With awareness, we can transform our health, finances and relationships by simply employing the power of the spoken word.

Ask yourself, "Are my words creating harmony or chaos in my life?"
Your answer holds the key to your transformation.

Become aware of your verbal patterns. Only then can you release the words keeping you "stuck" and replace them with ones that empower you physically, emotionally, mentally, financially and spiritually. If it feels overwhelming, take baby steps. Do a little bit each day. Remove at least three dis-empowering words from your vocabulary today. Replace them with three more empowering words. Tomorrow, choose three more. You ARE that powerful!

Pay attention to yourself. Notice the ideas and beliefs revealed in your conversations. Do they allow for greater success and a deeper connection with others? If not, this is your opportunity to make some changes. *As you change your vocabulary, you will change your results.* Your feelings will serve as a barometer. If a conversation leaves you feeling a sense of enthusiasm and joy, your words are serving you well. If a conversation leaves you drained, depleted, disconnected and misunderstood, you have the option to redesign your surroundings by changing your vocabulary.

People are often repetitive in their speech, with an *auto-pilot vocabulary leading them into the same "problems" over and over again!* Be aware of what you're saying, how you're saying it, as well as it's effectiveness. Are you generating the results you want? There are countless ways to improve the quality of your life and relationships by using different combinations of words.

Just as every action has a consequence,
every word generates a flow of energy

which is either beneficial or destructive.
You determine whether your energy
generates love or fear, connection or separation.

Verbal road blocks to your success feel heavy, like excess baggage. Replace them with the lighter, more empowering words which move on a higher frequency. As higher energy flows from you, you will improve your posture, breathing, and overall physiology. *Your body language will begin to align with the higher frequency of your words.*

Use words that create an attitude of gratitude, with a focus on abundance, wealth, and prosperity, and that is what your words will attract. Examples of words that tap directly into the ever-flowing stream of abundance are: lavish, infinite, flourishing, limitless, plentiful, thriving, rich, and bountiful. As you say them out loud, your energy field vibrates at a higher frequency.

Abundance, joy, love, bliss, gratitude, appreciation, and wisdom are all powerful high frequency words. *All of these powerful words are tied to FEELINGS, not physical things. The words generate feelings that attract resonant experiences.* So, when we select positive words, we naturally feel positive and attract rewarding experiences into our lives.

When we speak about lack and limitation, we depress ourselves and attract experiences that reinforce the feelings of lack and limitation. Wealth is an energy force we can tap into whenever we choose. Become the powerful creator you were meant to be! Liberate yourself today. *Tap into an infinite supply of abundance through the power of your thoughts, words, and feelings!*

The vibrations you send out will attract experiences on the same energy frequency. Maintain positive feelings and speak positive words. You will influence your environment positively because your surroundings always respond to your internal state of "being."

Joy-FULL conditions are created by a joy-FULL
internal state, and unhappy conditions are the result
of an unhappy or negative internal state.
Your internal state is revealed through your vocabulary.

Whenever you find yourself speaking negatively about money or abundance, shift your focus to say something more in tune with the things you WANT in your life.

It's application time!

Please take out your notebooks and title this exercise:

Creating My Soul Success Mantra!

A soul- success mantra is very personal. Select a personal success mantra that reflects the state of mind and way of being you aspire to.

Write it down and then *repeat, repeat, repeat.*
Repetition and consistency
will anchor this mantra in your subconscious mind.

The mantra becomes your fallback commentary in the deepest recesses of your mind. Place your mantra on sticky notes in your bathroom, car, refrigerator, desk, computer etc, until it takes root in your consciousness.

Examples of a soul success mantra are:

"Every day in every way my life gets better and better."
"In this moment, I make all things new!"
"Nothing disturbs my peace. I am always at peace."
"I am a magnet for millions."
"I am a champion creator."
"I generate success in all that I am and all that I do!"
"Beauty surrounds me at all times."

"I am now fulfilling my divine destiny."

"I am grateful for my success."

"I attract infinite opportunities for wealth, success and love."

"Everything good flows my way."

"Blissful surprises await me at every turn."

"I am an irresistible magnet for love, abundance and wealth beyond measure."

"All doors are open! An endless supply of abundance is mine."

"I am forever linked to an infinite flow of prosperity and love."

"Avalanches of abundance now come to me in perfect, divine ways."

"The floodgates of bliss and prosperity are now open!"

"I dwell in a sea of infinite abundance, serenity, inspiration and love."

There is no right or wrong way to select a mantra. Have fun with it, but remember the energy contained in your words.

Whatever you declare, you will attract!
Choose words that will attract success and abundance into your life!

Notice your world getting better and better with each passing day. When you consciously choose words that empower you life becomes extraordinary! ***You will shift from ordinary living into extraordinary living!*** You will realize that true prosperity and abundance emanates from within. Finally, eliminate the ineffective habit of chasing prosperity from the outside- in, so you will know the true meaning of INNER PEACE and prosperity.

We live in a world of language and energy. Words come alive, like living organisms, capable of expanding, changing, and influencing our world in powerful ways. ***With awareness, our words empower. Without awareness, they can easily imprison us in negative cycles of behavior and want.*** Our challenge is to take responsibility for our creative power, acknowledge the impact of our current communication patterns, and make the necessary changes to allow for the success, health, wealth and connection that is our birthright.

23. Create Wellness
(It's an Inside Job!)

⚜ Are you ready to experience the *radiant health, balance, and joy* that flows from the inside-out?

⚜ Are you ready to create a renewed sense of *vitality, contentment and inner peace*?

You are INTENDED to experience well-being. You generate wellness the same way you generate illness. It begins within. Your thoughts and emotions lay the groundwork for your outer experience. It is helpful to let go of the term "healing" all together. It is unproductive at best because it directs your attention to an illness you need to overcome. It places your predominant focus on battling what you fear instead of promoting what you desire.

> *The fastest way to wellness is to stop amplifying your struggles and shift your attention to generating wellness.*

When you consciously detach from the specific details of your disease and release the repetitively shared stories of limitation, you free your focus. From this space of clarity, you can write and tell a new empowered story that reflects the radiance and vitality you desire.

You are a vibrational being living in a vibrational universe. Your consciousness creates your life, so your body can re-balance at any time. Optimal health is your birthright. You deserve radiant, perfect health and wholeness! But, *you must be willing to take responsibility for yourself and your life* if you wish to experience this for yourself.

> *Wellness is a spiritual journey of first remembering*
> *and then awakening to your wholeness.*

The vital first step is ***claiming your power.*** Your emotions, thoughts, and spiritual awareness are vital components in determining the state of your body's health. A commitment to balancing your body, mind, and spirit will restore the proper energy flow in your body. You are meant to enjoy harmony within yourself. You have more power than you realize.

A shift in vibration that leads to wellness doesn't come from someone or something outside of you. It is an internal process of regeneration. ***Creating wellness in an inside-out job*** that may require changes in your lifestyle, habits, thoughts, beliefs and surroundings, but every effort to make these changes is worth its weight in gold.

It's important to understand the way your body communicates with you. The words it uses are your aches, pains and physical symptoms. They are your body's way of saying it needs attention, care and nurturing. If you reach for medicine to mask the symptoms before addressing the causes, you are telling your body to "shut up!" Illness is simply a vibrational indicator (rooted in resistance) revealing an lack of alignment with who you are. Once you shift the indicator, you shift into wellness.

We are traditionally taught that imbalances like cancer, diabetes, and allergies are hereditary conditions. Due to these limiting beliefs, we often feel like victims of our environment or prisoners of our genes. If we believe we have no power over dis-ease or ill health, we sadly forfeit our power to control our health. It's important to reclaim our power, to open the lines of communication with our bodies, and to identify the sources of our symptoms.

> ***It's time to start looking for vibrational causes rather than cures!***
> ***The root of our illnesses and dis-ease lies within us.***
> ***Long-standing, chronic negative emotion is***
> ***the basis for almost all dis-ease.***

Problems we suppress, deny or disconnect from create imbalances in our energy fields. Refusing to address these problems causes them to surface in the form of physical symptoms. ***The purpose of a physical symptom (pain or discomfort) is to notify you*** that you have disconnected from an experience on a subconscious level (usually due to emotional disruption or chaos) and this disconnection has created an imbalance in your body.

Repressed or chaotic emotions are trapped in a holding pattern inside you. But symptoms can be gifts, your greatest ally in reestablishing internal harmony. ***Symptoms are doorways*** through which you reconnect with repressed emotions until you regain balance and heal your body. ***Emotions are simply energy in motion.*** When the motion is blocked, the cause must be addressed so the emotions can flow again.

Expressing stuck emotions is vital. You can do this through journaling, meditation, intention and forgiveness. You do not have to re-live an old experience to get the energy flowing again. This is about conscious release. Until you acknowledge and release your repressed emotions, limiting beliefs will inhibit you from remembering your power to create vibrant health. When you confront your stuck emotions, simply use your power to consciously release the associated limiting belief or trauma and begin to heal.

It's application time again!

Please take out your notebooks and title these exercises:

Tools for Self Healing.

You can shift illness into wellness and dis-ease into ease using the frequencies of abundance, harmony and peace. You can dwell in a self-regenerating, self-rejuvenating, disease-FREE and ageless body!

Visualization, Meditation and Affirmations are three powerful and effective tools for generating momentum for well-being.

> *Practice one of more of these exercises daily to assist you*
> *in your journey to radiant health and wellness.*

Reclaiming your power to experience vibrancy is your birthright! Write down the affirmations that resonate with you and integrate them into your everyday routine.

Affirmations for Self Healing:

Thoughts are alive. *Words are crystallized thoughts with immeasurable power*, especially when spoken with deliberate and conscious intention.

First, say the affirmations out loud to *command the full attention of your conscious mind.* Then repeat them silently until you feel your energy is on the same frequency as the words.

Continue repeating the words until they they are anchored into all levels of your being. By repeating the affirmations, and taking inspired action based on the feelings they generate, you strengthen your awareness of the health you desire. And, the words' energy remain with you as you move through your day.

- I nourish myself with healing foods every day to satisfy and completely heal my mind, body, and spirit.
- I deserve vibrant health and wellness in my life right now, and will not accept less.
- I love myself completely and take excellent care of my heart, mind, body, and spirit.
- I am totally safe and surrounded by love, light, peace, and joy.
- I am completely relaxed and my mind, body and spirit are peaceful and calm. All is wonderful in my life.
- Every day, in every way, my life gets better and better.
- I let go of all that I no longer need. My body is healing quickly and easily.

⅄ My past is over and I release it. I live in the present with happiness, love, and joy.

⅄ I believe in my power to generate wellness. My body, mind and spirit know exactly what to do and how to function for optimum health. I surrender, let go and trust my higher guidance to show me the way.

⅄ I am in radiant perfect health and my body is perfect in every way. I am looking and feeling more youthful and vibrant each day.

⅄ I rest easily and peacefully every night, knowing my body is regenerating while I sleep.

⅄ I have abundant energy and a strong healthy immune system. I am whole and complete just as I am.

⅄ I am consistently moving in tune with the frequency of abundance, harmony and peace. My body is self-regenerating, disease-free, ageless and whole.

VISUALIZATION/MEDITATION TECHNIQUE FOR CREATING WELLNESS:

White Light Spiral Rejuvenation Flush

This technique has powerful and immediate benefits. The use of light energy regenerates your body. The light isn't physical light – its an etheric substance emanating from God, the divine source of all creation. It has numerous levels of colors in its spectrum. You can summon it every day through intention and visualization to *awaken, revive, rejuvenate, and balance your energy field.*

Connecting with this light is simple and easy. You call upon it verbally or silently, or by visualizing. The activation occurs through the divine power of your will and intention. Even a verbal command as simple as "I now surround myself with white light" or "I now summon the white light to saturate every cell in my body with divine love" begins the process.

When you call upon this light, it shows up. All you have to do is take a few minutes each day to center and align your energy by activating this technique called the *WHITE LIGHT SPIRAL REJUVENATION FLUSH!*

> *This process relieves stress by re-balancing,*
> *recalibrating and grounding your energy through the*
> *power of intention and mental projection.*
> *It works like a prayer or an invocation.*

It is most effective when practiced on a daily basis, so your energy systems and intuitive abilities continue running at their optimum levels. You can do it during meditation, while having your tea or coffee in the morning, or even in the shower. There is no wrong time or wrong way to do this!

To begin, take a few deep cleansing breaths, in through the nose and out through the mouth. Breathe in to a count of three and out to a count of three. Continue this conscious breathing throughout the process.

1. Set the intention silently or verbally to call upon God, your higher self, and your spiritual team of light. Connect with the cellular intelligence within your physical body. Take another deep full cleansing breath, in through the nose and out through the mouth.

2. Visualize a column of white light streaming in from the heavenly realms, coming in through the top of your head (your crown chakra.) Visualize this light spiraling vertically through the center of your body down through the soles of your feet. See this light streaming down in a spiral formation through every cell and molecule, flushing through your entire energy field. This light will strengthen your entire energy field.

3. Allow this beautiful white light to speed up as it spirals through your energy field, purifying, rejuvenating, and rebalancing your cells, meridians and chakras. The spiraling motion of this divine white light unlocks all density within your energy field, loosening any low-frequency "stuck" energy within your physical, mental, emotional, and etheric bodies. Your stuck energy is then transformed into light.

4. Take a few more full deep breaths, in through the nose and out through your mouth. As you breathe in and out, you break up more and more dense energy stored in your cells and energy field. With each breathe, white light continues to spiral through your entire energy field, clearing debris, and transforming it into light. Keep breathing and visualizing this divine white light spiraling through you, revitalizing you in miraculous ways.

5. Visualize the white light stabilizing as the spiraling slows down. This final part of the flushing process clears the path for your day to begin. Now, project this beautiful, radiant white light outward. See it expanding in front of you, creating a clear pathway of divine light surrounding you and permeating every place you go today. Intend for it. Feel it. See it. Know it's happening.

6. You are a now a beacon of light; a divine lighthouse radiating love, joy and beauty. Take a few more full deep breaths, in for a count of three and out for a count of three. Anchor the light in your energy field by setting the intention and visualizing it happening.

7. Take one more deep breath, in through the nose and out through the mouth. The process is now complete. Open your eyes, wiggle your fingers and toes, roll your shoulders, and feel yourself fully grounded in the earth. Feel roots stemming

from the soles of your feet to firmly ground you into this beautiful physical reality. Now move through the rest of your day feeling centered. Thank your spiritual support team for their assistance, and move into your day, a divine beacon of light.

The process is relatively simple and quick. Apply this process daily, and you will be well on your way to experiencing greater health, harmony, inspiration and peace. ***This is a gift you give yourself, moving from suppression to expression, affirming your radiant health, nurturing yourself*** through meditation and visualization. The reward is the quality of your day to day existence.

Are you ready to make changes to immeasurably enhance the quality of your life? Take responsibility for nurturing your heart, body, mind, and spirit. ***Health and wellness follow when you release your pain, shifting yourself into a positive state of "being."***

Take control of your health by eating foods that give you strength, energy, and vitality. Exercise regularly to maintain strong energy flows in your body. Let go of stressful relationships or jobs that no longer serve you. Choose to honor yourself fully.

> ***Creating wellness is simply a process of becoming "whole" again, a process of awakening and examining yourself in an honest, complete way. Your entire being plays a role in your health, not just the physical aspect.***

With deliberate focus and conscious choices, you can ***break free of any limiting patterns*** which prevent you from feeling whole, complete, rejuvenated, vibrant, liberated, and FREE.

Choose to transcend anything keeping you from experiencing joy, radiant health, prosperity, and inner peace. Realize you don't have to struggle or fight your way through life anymore. ***The intensity of the***

chaos and discontent is self-inflicted. Lighten your load by exercising your power to release any attachment to the drama. Rise above the dark clouds of negativity and move into the light of awareness. You have the power to choose harmony, to transcend the heaviness.

Remember, the way you respond to your challenges plays a significant role in your health. Any subconscious, limiting reactions rooted in pessimistic thoughts, feelings and beliefs will result in stagnant energy flows within your cells. This is precisely what leads to physical symptoms and dis-ease. When you respond to life with love, faith and gratitude, your experience is transformed, your health improves and you know inner peace.

Your health challenges are divinely designed invitations to claim your power. Any barriers separating you from vibrant health can be dissolved with conscious effort and desire.

Consistently forgive yourself and others, release stuck energy and repressed emotions, and choose love over fear.

The barriers melt away, **and your health improves.**
The challenges you face are simply hidden jewels leading to expansion.

Your health is not out of your hands! Commit to generating wellness in thought, word and action and you will experience the vibrancy, and wholeness that is your birthright.

24. SACRED GEOMETRY

After my near death experience, I had a series of dreams in which I saw images in an etheric script of shapes, symbols and colors. This is a universal language called "The Language of Light" and all humans know it at our core.

The multi-dimensional wisdom encoded in the images generate beautiful healing and positive change. The images and their related tones are energetic keys we understand in our hearts. They are not intended to be understood by the analytical mind, but rather physically, emotionally, mentally and spiritually. *This living language of light employs light, color and sacred geometry to create healing.* The symbols and resulting messages are conduits to higher awareness.

Many other beautiful souls on the planet know this universal language. Some can transmit the light language and its frequencies through their voices. Others replay it with their hands and emit invisible flashes of light in geometric patterns, codes and colors. The symbols and tones of the language of light are interwoven with sacred geometry that vibrates on divine light frequencies. *This is a sacred, living language understood in the cells of our bodies, and it opens a clear channel to our divine heritage and galactic family. The language of light allows us to evolve into our true and infinite selves.*

The universal codes help us remember who we are, aligning us with our divinity, acting as our connection to source energy. *The codes activate our original, although dormant,* 12 strands of DNA. How can the language of light activate DNA? The structure of our human body is based on the same set of principles found in all creation.

*Our bodies contain all the information of the universe,
because we are an embodiment of sacred geometry.
We are spirit and matter combined!*

The language or light and its sacred geometric symbols allow us to interact with divine energy fields which emit energy at a frequency that awakens our dormant DNA.

There is one primary universal light language, but many variations vibrate at different frequencies. These light languages sound like ancient earth languages with overtones of Aramaic, Egyptian, Chinese, Indian, Hebrew, Tibetan, Native American, Polynesian and others. For the human brain, it feels a bit odd at first, like listening to a foreigner speak. It can also be more tonal, like dolphin or whale sounds.

The sacred language of creation cannot be mastered by rote learning. Its multi-dimensional vibrations expand outward into form, and its *divinely encoded information cannot be translated by the analytical mind.* The Language of Light is our link to Source Creation. In the higher realms, it is an integration of geometry and light rays, while in the middle realms it is sounds on different frequencies. These sounds provided the foundation for the ancient languages, from which our newer languages evolved. *The Language of Light is uncorrupted; it is pure light.*

What makes geometry "sacred?"

Sacred Geometry is comprised of shapes, colors, vibrations and sounds. Plato said, "every piece of matter breaks down into specific geometric shapes". Sacred geometry is the vehicle on which Spirit brings energy into the physical plane, transforming thought into matter. It is the Divine, as represented by forms and shapes. *It marries heaven and earth, physical reality merging into the energy of the Sacred.* It is the Architecture of Creation.

Repeating geometric patterns are the basic building blocks of our material world, from our physical bodies, plants and animals, to planets, stars, and galaxies. We find these patterns of creation throughout nature: in crystals, tree branches, snowflakes, pine cones, honeycombs, flower petals, sea shells, a sunflower center, the double helix of our DNA, the cornea of an eye, our own spiraling galaxy! ***The entire universe is a series of geometric designs, repeating over and over in endless dances of sound, light and color.***

We comprehend this Language of Light at different levels of our being. Its patterns combine math, which is understood by our logical left brain, and beauty, which is appreciated by our creative right brain.

> ***Sacred Geometry unites the mind and heart,***
> ***spirit and matter, science and spirituality.***

The purpose of the language of light is personal and planetary healing through messages encoded with layers of divine information. ***It awakens and inspires higher consciousness on earth***. *Each positive step in our personal evolution speeds up the evolution of the planet as a whole.* ***The universal language interacts with our energetic systems to implement our divine blueprints*** *and realize our greatest soul potential.*

All living forms are sacred energy in constant motions of color and sound. Each shape vibrates at it's own unique frequency, so a cube has a different purpose or effect than a pyramid or tetrahedron. Sacred Geometry is divine intelligence, a collection of universal experiences communicating vast amounts of information. *This language of light raises our own frequencies,* creating patterns of consciousness which unite us with all things and awaken the sacred within us.

> ***These exquisite patterns are inter-dimensional doorways***
> ***to the wonder of the eternal and the divine.***

Each sacred geometric shape possesses a particular energy. **Sacred geometry forms your aura,** which you create with light, vibration, and sound. Our chakras emit sacred shapes in various shades of colored light, forming auras which continuously change in response to our thoughts and feelings. Each aura connects with other people as well as the energy grid of the planet, attracting events into our lives which *are in tune with our deeper selves.* Light language and its sacred geometry has the power to heal the subconscious mind, bringing opportunities we could not conceive of on a conscious level.

> **Sacred geometry confirms the ancient truth**
> **that all life evolves from the same blueprint,**
> **the same source: the ever-present,**
> **unconditionally loving creative force many of us call "God."**

This geometry is the key to a broader understanding of the universe, making all aspects of reality sacred. The ancient civilizations of the Egyptians, Mayans, Sirians, Atlanteans, and Lemurians knew this truth and so incorporated sacred geometry into their priestly schools.

Sacred geometry can be used by each of us to see the unity of all life, and to connect more fully with each other and the Universe. This divine math is a tool for spiritual, mental, emotional and physical healing, bringing inner peace and harmony through expressions of unity and love. **Once these truths are understood by the mind (left brain) and experienced through the heart (right brain), a whole new world comes alive!**

Language is how we communicate with each other.

The Language of Light is how we and God communicate with each other. Our souls interpret the symbols, so the light language can expand our awareness of the grander picture. We receive universal information in holographic light packets which remain in our energy fields like time release capsules. We absorb the information as we are ready for it. These codes and their associated frequencies also stay in our energy fields for the benefit of others. We become beacons of light, emitting high frequency light programs for others as we simply go about our day-to-day lives.

We are all connected, whether we realize it or not.

The language of light creates some very practical benefits:

Wellness, rejuvenation, expanded awareness: The language of light dissolves resistance, accelerating a return to healthy body functions and vitality. With your energy field cleansed, higher light programs lead to renewal, regeneration and redefinition, resulting in greater passion, enthusiasm and radiance.

Release Blocks to Your Personal Healing: The images and sounds of the light language release old blockages to make your body receptive to multi-dimensioanl healing.

Accelerated Spiritual Evolution: The language's multidimensional energy codes accelerate your soul's evolution by raising your energetic vibrations to a higher frequency. This creates expanded awareness.

Cellular Re-patterning and Enhanced Psychic Awareness: The Language of Light is a pure communication of divinely encoded messages. This leads to healing at the deepest levels , to cellular re-patterning and expanded consciousness.

It's application time!

Please take out your notebooks and title this exercise:

My Left and Right Brain AND the Language of Light

Since the language of light is multi-dimensional, and cannot be understood by the linear, 3D mind, our right brain needs no reconditioning. It already understands the language of light! It already flows with the energy of creation. But our left brain knows only matter, logic, reason, analysis, black and white. What it can see, it will believe. What it can hear, it will understand. So, the left brain needs a little reconditioning.

That reconditioning involves using sacred geometry in a practical way. We must learn the power of drawing the sacred geometric figures. When you write or draw, your left brain takes over. It works in logical sequences so you know that A comes before B and not vice-versa. Your left brain guides even the most creative piece of poetry throughout the actual writing process. The poetry was formed by the right brain, but putting it down on paper is the task of the left brain. So, we must condition the left brain by drawing sacred geometric figures.

Sacred geometry depicts universal energy.

Each shape and structure carries a different energy, sound, color, and tone. **So, begin by drawing the basic sacred geometric shapes. Nothing complicated, nothing complex!** All the complex sacred geometric shapes are formed by putting the basic shapes together.

Begin with a shape you know, the shape of the cosmos: A circle is the energy of completion, of wholeness, the energy of life itself. Keep drawing the circle, again and again and again. This cannot be a mental activity. It must be done physically. A circle has no beginning and no end, just like the universe.

You won't need a compass because sacred geometry is free-flowing. Do not bind it. Draw a circle, again and again and again. You might draw two circles, one next to the other. You may want to go over it, again and again. Whatever you wish to do, DO! Get lost in the activity; **turn it into a meditation**. This is how you recondition your left brain.

While meditating, your left brain tries to unite with your right brain. So get lost in the circle or whatever geometric shape you are drawing. Allow the shape to pull you in, to activate both sides of your brain: awareness in your left brain and consciousness in your right brain. Eventually, the two sides unite. You will remain lost in consciousness while still completely aware physically. *The the ego and spirit merge into a moment when neither dominates.* (This exercise is especially important if you feel your analytical masculine energy is stronger than your feminine creative energy.)

The feminine energy is not only a circle, but a spiral. Unlike a circle, a spiral goes on and on, starting from the very center, moving outward in concentric rings on its infinite journey. *The spiral is our journey of evolution*. From the center, from the Source, creation begins and expands. The energy of the source is never interrupted because the spiral is endless.

The spiral is evolution of feminine energy: an ongoing creative process. It always moves outward, letting go, and surrendering its past. Anytime you feel past memories keeping you stuck, start drawing the spiral to take yourself away from the past. Likewise, if you need to go back, to resolve or harmonize a past experience, draw a reverse spiral. Use this reverse spiral to revisit the trauma, to surrender to it, let it go, to release yourself from the connection. Think of the trauma as you draw. When you feel resolution, stop and draw a normal spiral, saying: "I am letting it go. I surrender. I am evolving." *The spiral is about expansion, just as the reverse spiral is about contraction. Sometimes contraction is necessary to eliminate the negative energy of a traumatic experience*. So never be afraid to draw the reverse spiral to harmonize your energy and resume your journey with more grace and ease.

You've drawn two sacred geometric shapes representing the feminine energy. *Now, we come to the masculine energy, the square*. We have a saying in our society: "don't be square!" It means, don't be dull, lackluster, or lack creativity. The square is masculine energy. It does not have the energy of creation. With that said, the square is very important because it brings structure and order.

When disorder reigns within or around you, you need structure. The sacred geometric shape you must draw is the square. Draw it again and again in whatever way you like. There is no right or wrong way to do this.

And now.... *draw a shape which balances yin and yang: the cross. The cross is the sacred symbol of the balance between spirit and matter, between feminine and masculine*. But the cross is significant in another way, as well. It is the sacred figure of transition, transformation, optimism, cheer, happiness and hope. Many associate the cross with Jesus, and if there was one message he gave us, it is that all is not lost. The cross reminds us that nothing, not even death, can bring the end of all that is good and true and joyous. So when you're feeling down, draw the cross. When you need to balance the left and the right brain, the yin and the yang, draw the cross. As you move into balance, you will move closer to the next stage of your evolution.

This next symbol is loved by most women— the heart. We love drawing hearts! Young girls could spend the entire day drawing hearts in their books and on their papers. What they are actually doing is practicing sacred geometry. To bring sensitivity, draw the heart. To understand your emotions, to understand the emotions of others, draw the heart. To move from conditional love to unconditional love, draw the heart.

The diamond is a very sacred symbol as well; the symbol of ascension, growth, and clarity. *The diamond offers YOU clarity.* When you are confused, in need of direction, draw a diamond. It not only brings clarity, it helps you connect to your intuition, so your direction becomes soul-driven.

The triangle is the symbol of unity, oneness, balance, and the creativity that comes from balance. It is the symbol of manifestation, illumination, magic and alchemy!

These shapes are a few of the basic sacred geometric codes and the energies they contain. Use these! Use them for yourself. Anyone can draw these shapes. ***You don't have to be overwhelmed or frightened by the complexity of sacred geometry!*** Once you've had some fun with these basic shapes, create your own composite sacred shapes! For example, you could put triangle upon triangle upon triangle upon triangle to create the flower of life. Create whatever shapes you desire. What is the combination of energy you are looking for?

Once you have mastered the basic shapes and understand their energy, you will accomplish more complex shapes quite naturally. You will flow into it. First, work with the individual shapes, then proceed to design your own sacred geometry, which is truly your language of creation. ***Everything on Earth is formed by sacred geometry.*** I wish you happy drawing!

Enjoy the journey of re-discovering the real "you."

25. ELIXIR OF ETERNAL YOUTH

We all have the right to experience heaven on earth! I've coached men and women from all walks of life, and whether they are business owners, healers, teachers, doctors, bankers, actors, writers, homemakers or celebrities, they all want the same things: an energetic, youthful body with radiant skin, taut, toned limbs and a sense of vitality when they wake up each day! We truly can feel rested, appear luminous, and feel peaceful within because this is our divine birthright.

> *We are dynamic, vibrational beings capable of*
> *accessing an infinite supply of life force energy.*

One of the benefits of age is the wisdom from greater life experiences. *However, the 'baggage' our bodies accumulate at a cellular level (from a lifetime of trauma and drama) can negatively affect our ability to enjoy those benefits!* Most healthcare systems treat symptoms, but do not address the root causes. Symptoms are temporarily eliminated, but return because the cause of the problem was not addressed. Once symptoms become chronic, they are more challenging to reverse, so finding the cause is more important than ever.

Acute symptoms are your body's way of communicating with you, so don't prolong your misery! You have the power to feel better and become whole again.

> *Your body is a self rejuvenating organism, and optimal health*
> *depends on adopting new empowering beliefs, a consistently*
> *held state of positive expectancy, daily self nurturing*
> *practices, cellular regeneration, and detoxification.*

You must cleanse your body of the accumulated toxins which have settled in your organs and tissues over the years. Pay attention to what your body is communicating, and trust your ability to make yourself whole again. You will experience the rejuvenation that is your divine birthright.

Despite most of the health information we receive from traditional media outlets, our bodies are not destined to grow increasingly fragile with age. ***Our bodies are extremely resilient and fully capable of rejuvenating themselves!*** The body's cells are in a constant state of renewal, as old cells are discarded and new ones created in their place. Each type of tissue has its own turnover time, depending in part on the workload endured by its cells. Couple this knowledge with an understanding of our divine blueprints, and we can channel our bodies energy to ***turn back the clock and regenerate all of the bodies' systems!***

You will look more radiant, beautiful, healthy and youthful by honoring your divine blueprint and remembering your ability to consciously create your reality. You can control your health and extend your lifespan because each of us has the ability to extend our physical limits!

We were born to become walking, talking, living miracles, conscious pioneers as we merge the physical and spiritual.

Do you want to inhabit a self-rejuvenating, self-regenerating, ageless body?

Do you want to experience markedly increased energy, improved endurance, improved sleep patterns, a calmer disposition, increased clarity and natural healing throughout your body?

Your belief system holds the key. As you believe, so shall you be! Limiting thoughts and beliefs promote illness, aging and death and stop us from enjoying eternal youth.

Would you like to create a body free of illness, dis-ease and limitation? Most diseases are caused by mental and emotional stress inhabiting your energy field.

> *Stress is caused by imbalanced, fearful attitudes and beliefs which eventually become physical symptoms. These symptoms, when ignored or suppressed with medicine alone, lead to disease.*

Everyday tension, dispassionate living, financial and relationship anxieties, as well as the toxicity of emotional pain, anger and resentment block the flow of our energy fields. The stagnation of the energetic and physical pathways clog up the natural flow of life-force energy and leads to dis-ease. The beauty is that the solution can be very simple! Remove the obstructions and become whole again!

No amount of money, vitamins, powders, shakes, creams, hormones or b12 shots will ever make you feel the vibrancy that is your divine birthright! You simply cannot buy life-force energy. When you remove the physical, emotional, and energetic imbalances a little more each day, you will naturally allow a resurgence of fresh-flowing life-force energy throughout your body that will fuel you with a brand new sense of vitality – generated from the inside-out!

Spiritual energy healing will also clear negative cellular memory. Each of our cells has a consciousness, which is influenced positively or negatively by thought. When our thoughts are combined with strong intention and specific techniques, we can direct powerful waves of energy to alter the information in the cells and produce positive new results!

Disease, aging and death are ancient thoughts implanted in our consciousness. We are highly creative and powerful beings!

> *The body is the 'temple of the soul' and our divine potential allows us to transform our bodies at anytime.*

> *We rejuvenate when we trust our bodies innate
> capacity to guide us back to wholeness.*

Multi-dimensional awareness allows us to move beyond legacies of limitation. This is part of our evolution as souls here on earth. To upgrade our consciousness and physical bodies, our souls must clear the bodies' mental and emotional distortions to bring us back into alignment with our original divine blueprints. You can achieve this through **daily intention, meditation, self nurturing patterns and habits,** but it must be a committed daily regimen.

When we first become aware of ourselves as multi-dimensional beings, we realize we have accumulated many attitudes and beliefs which are not in harmony with our blueprints. *These attitudes create toxic energies that must be cleared so our bodies can refocus on our original blueprints.* This occurs when we enhance the flow of life force energy within our bodies with deliberate intention and conscious, inspired action.

Develop a **daily discipline, including meditation, visualization, and connection with your spiritual support team to assist this clearing process.** This routine will guide your thoughts, words and actions, allowing you to achieve your highest potential while preventing many unnecessary years of suffering and drama. Learn to manage your energy by taking a few moments between daily tasks to balance your energy field. Choose a meditation technique and do it each day until it becomes second nature. Consistency is the key.

> *Practice shifting from the go-go-go mentality
> to pauses which balance, ground and center you.*

The purpose in integrating these tools into your daily practice is to increase the flow of harmonious energy in your body. In order for your own life force energy to transform you, it must flow as freely, easily, and rapidly as possible throughout your body.

They key is removing the obstructions (mental, emotional and physical) that prevent optimal life force energy from flowing through your energy field easily, like a swiftly running river. The primary intention with any of these daily disciplines is to **create a body that operates with a clear, unobstructed flow!** Your body and your energy cannot be depleted when fresh life-force energy is consistently flowing through it. You could consider this ever-present, always available life-force energy as your very own fountain of youth! Yet, the only way to access the fountain is allowing the free flow of this energy as often as possible.

Be sure to get out in the fresh air and sunshine as often as possible!

Breathe consciously and deeply to oxygenate and re-balance your energy as often as possible! Shallow breathing can lead to premature again and even premature death! Why? Because when your breathing lacks power, your circulation slows down and everything stagnates.

> **Take twenty deep, consciously long breaths**
> **(in through the nose and out through the**
> **mouth) each morning and evening.**
> This helps clear any stress and "stuck"
> energy lodged inside your body.

Replace stress with laughter as often as possible!

Another way to increase the flow is the following grounding meditation. It is a simple, easy practice that involves visualizing a straight line of white light coming in through the top of your head and running all the way to the soles of your feet. **Imagine this light stabilizing and grounding you while settling any imbalanced thoughts or emotions.** This technique is quick, easy and highly effective in keeping your body in a state of harmony. By focusing through visualization and meditation, you direct the flow of energy to your body's own healing capacities, thereby restoring and rejuvenating yourself.

It's also very important to regularly practice some kind of full body movement to keep your energy flowing harmoniously. Walking, dancing, tai chi, yoga, pilates, aerobic workouts, or running help calibrate the various energy frequencies in your body. Taking nature walks and interacting with animals also boost your energy. Regular massage, chiropractic or acupuncture treatments help reduce other energy imbalances and *generate a renewed sense of fluidity – the trump card of optimal health!* Any body holds the potential, regardless of age, of achieving a youth-full leanness, sense of fluidity, and renewed vitality.

> *The key is shaking up the stale energy and enlivening your body by deliberately and consciously circulating pure life-force energy!*

Cellular memory is an important quantum concept that must be understood and integrated into our awareness. *Every cell in our bodies carries memories from all our past experiences.* Positive memories assist our bodies in reaching their full potential, but cells can also hold traumatic memories. Often times we experience a sudden physical symptom without knowing it is associated with a negative past experience.

Irrational phobias, food allergies or sudden physical problems are often due to a negative cellular memory. In many cases, we can neutralize these negative memories through meditation, intention, or hypnosis. We need not relive emotional or physical trauma to move past it. We must simply focus on releasing the negative memory from the affected cells by directing these cells' energy to vibrate at a higher frequency. With intention, these cells return to health. Intentionality is the key to transformation.

Using the power of focus and intention, you will experience wholeness. Once aware of a current symptom/ailment, connect with your higher self and spiritual support team. State the following intention: "I fully release this negative cellular memory." *Complete this process by visualizing the affected cells being saturated with light, flushing out the negative memory.* Cellular regeneration is a natural and gradual process beginning with the body receiving increased amounts of light from the higher dimensions.

You can also use your power of intention to release memories of pain, suffering, disease and degeneration trapped in your energy field.

Visualize all the cells in your body vibrating more and more quickly. See each cell emitting pure light into its surrounding cells, creating a chain reaction through your entire body.

It is entirely possible to radically improve your overall life experience, revitalize your energy field, create a free flowing internal system, create a more attractive appearance, release your body from block-ages, release stress, recharge your cells with enlivened health, and experience new surges of energy and bliss, by *choosing to fill your body with high vibration foods.*

The foods we consume on a daily basis either rapidly deplete OR invigorate us!

Low vibration foods and substances are typically dense and slow to move through the body They include mainstream processed foods, synthetic ingredients, cigarettes, hard liquor, animal flesh, pharma-ceutical drugs etc. A steady diet of low vibration diet filled with processed, refined and synthetic foods throws the body completely out of whack! This is because they are difficult to break down AND because the chemical reactions that take place as these substances struggle to move through our bloodstream and intestines makes us moody, bloated, lethargic and just plain grumpy at times. That kind of lifestyle depletes us of vital life force energy.

On the other hand, *high vibrational foods are light-filled, hydrating, and move rapidly through the body.* High life force energy foods are full of light that comes directly from the sun! They are grown closest to the sun, so as we consume them we bring that powerful energy into our energy fields, thereby raising our body's vibrations. The intention is to choose foods that offer the greatest amounts of life force energy, that are most harmonious with our natural vibration, and that contribute more life energy than take it!

A combination of adopting a healthy, "high-vibe" diet, committing to intentional, positive living, coupled with self nurturing routines that include consistent exercise, regular meditation, and empowering visualization will enliven your body, from the inside-out.

Your vitality is directly linked to the natural flow of life force energy within your body. A deliberately created unobstructed flow produces a powerful sense of inner ecstasy. This inner ecstasy is a result of that free-flowing vitality, AND it IS the SOURCE of the seemingly elusive, yet always available fountain of youth.

Overall well being is the goal.

It's application time again!

Please take out your notebooks and title this exercise:

Creating My own Personal Healing Temple.

Please commit to the following steps.

1. Set time aside each day to create your own healing temple with the power of your imagination and intention.

2. Before going to sleep each night, visualize yourself entering a beautiful room containing a large bed in the center. This bed holds energies designed specifically for your healing and rejuvenation.

3. See yourself lying down on this beautiful bed, knowing you created this temple for yourself. Feel the peace, serenity and positive energy. Look around you and see flowers, crystals and flowing water increasing your serenity. ***This is where your body will rest and recover from all the stresses of your day.*** Only the highest vibrations of love and light should enter this space. Relax to release all tension.

4. Visualize white light filling the entire room, knowing you are safe and protected. Hear soft music and see beautiful waves of color gently enfolding you.

5. Remain here as long as you like. ***This is your personal healing temple.*** Each night, visit your healing temple to ask your guardian angel and spiritual support team to assure a quiet and peaceful night of sleep.

Always remember your power to create vibrant health through positive intentions. ***Demand physical perfection, trust your creative potential, and expect miracles!*** Develop you own healing affirmations, and listen to your body as it communicates with you each day. Drink plenty of water and visualize it washing away stress. Ask your spiritual support team to assist you in releasing all remaining thought or behavior patterns which no longer serve your highest good.

With awareness, attention, and practice, you will reclaim your ancient healing powers.

You are a natural self-healer, so tap into your infinite potential.
It is your divine birthright, your personal passport to wholeness.
Will you claim it?

26. THRIVE

My fondest wish is that your journey through this book will help you increase the depth and richness of your daily experience! My greatest intention is that YOU will remember your power and allow the magic to happen!

You are not small, insignificant, or power-less.
You are a multidimensional, eternal, powerful being,
and your soul's blueprint will guide you
through your divine mission on this planet.

It's time for YOU to live with a renewed sense of fascination and awe, and activate your eternal light every day! You have a divine right to be the conscious creator of your life, so shift out of survival mode and start to THRIVE. Move through the portal into limitless prosperity and an unstoppable flow of abundance. Your birthright is true soul-driven success!

The power to thrive lies within.
With all due respect and compassion,
I must say... "stop letting life happen TO you"!

From this moment forward, consciously determine the quality of your experience. Never forget your innate power to generate extraordinary success in every area of your life.

The "heavenly treasures" shared in this book
are designed to expand your awareness
about who you are, why you're here, and what's possible for you.

As you apply the information, you will become an irresistible magnet for the people, inspirations and opportunities that are perfectly aligned with your soul. Choose to create this powerful change.

Remember, the external world alone cannot give you anything of lasting value because its rewards are fleeting. The world around you reflects only what you give yourself. Beginning today, become *independent of objects, people and events. Everything you need already exists inside you. Discover self-love. Remember your magnificence.* Find the glory beyond the roles you play – beyond the drama – so you can dance to the melody of life with passion, enthusiasm, rhythm, joy, and vibrancy! Spiritual amnesia began when you were born so you forgot your radiance and power. It's time to move beyond the limitations of the past, into a lifestyle befitting your soul's brilliance.

Today is the first day of the rest of your amazing life! *Stop surviving and start thriving.* Embrace your innate creative potential. *There are two primary ways to re-inject wonder and awe into your life.* One is to see with fresh eyes, to notice the expansive light of your inner self from a grander perspective. The other is to tap into your innate potential, to evolve, succeed, and expand throughout the adventure of your life.

You were born to thrive. Although you will encounter many challenges along the way, you have the power to decide how long and painful these challenges will be. Life is a journey, and you will be strengthened by your struggles. You are a spiritual being temporarily inhabiting physical form, and you will thrive as you rise above your challenges to learn your soul lessons!

You are meant to expand, grow and evolve. Always remember the magnificence of your creative potential. Utilize your personal power to make your wildest dreams come true! These are the dreams your soul intended for you to experience in this lifetime.

Don't leave this life before you have danced
to all the music of your soul.
Project the music outward,
sharing the unique melody of your brilliance with the world.

To shift from surviving to thriving, you must broaden your perspective!

When you look at your experiences through a more expansive lens,
"obstacles" become opportunities,
and "hurdles" become stepping stones
to greater understanding, compassion, awareness and success.

Enjoy your role as a conscious creator! Creating wealth and success is first and foremost an inner game played in your mind. To thrive, you must fuel your mind by planting seeds of opportunity in your thoughts. Those seeds will grow into words, actions, and finally, success.

A primary obstacle is RESISTANCE to change. Stop resisting! Change must be a constant in life. It is how we evolve and grow. So, move through the twists and turns without resistance. Resisting the flow fuels frustration and keeps you stuck in a cycle of limitation. *What you resist will persist!* Resisting change is attempting to alter the natural order of the universe. Why not tell the seasons to stop changing or trees to stop growing? Don't let that happen in your life! Create unstoppable growth and success by getting out of our own way.

Early in your expansion, you may feel discomfort, but this feeling is simply a *a sign that you are moving out of old comfort zones!* Discomfort highlights internal growing pains as you stretch beyond past limitations and into a new, more expansive reality.

So please come to see discomfort as your invitation to spiritual expansion. Simply notice it. Then, *allow the resistance to flow right*

out of you. Don't prolong discomfort by trying to fight it or "figure it out." The biggest gift you give yourself is the willingness to "go with the flow." The initial discomfort is a natural part of evolution. When you stop fighting it, magic happens! Any path to power and purpose will stretch and challenge you. So, your initial resistance is something to be celebrated! Growth and success lie on the other side.

The comparison game is another common trap. ***There are no winners or losers, and it's not a race.*** Comparing your personal transformation or spiritual growth to other people's journeys is fruitless.

The following affirmation will anchor this truth in your consciousness:

> *"I AM succeeding on MY personal journey to wholeness*
> *at the perfect rate of speed for my spiritual evolution.*
> *I bless everyone around me,*
> *and realize we are all on unique journeys.*
> *I am responsible only for my own growth and expansion.*
> *Everyone changes at his own pace. It's not a race.*
> *It is not my job to change anyone else.*
> *My evolution is my only responsibility."*

Realize YOUR soul potential by activating your power to focus on the thoughts, words, actions and feelings that allow you to shift from surviving to thriving! This is your greatest gift to yourself. Thrive and take control of your future life. There is no better time than the present moment – start with a clean slate on which to print your new ideas, intentions and goals. Do things differently. If the patterns of your past haven't served you, create new, empowering, expansive, healthy, positive patterns in their place! Don't hold regrets about the past. It's over and done! ***Focusing on what's already happened only keeps you in survival mode.*** What you can control is your power, energy, focus and attention, all of which will contribute to a far more productive life.

Choose to consciously create your life, filling it with a sense of clarity, commitment, purpose, passion, and confidence. Create clear intentions for your phenomenal life. ***Embrace your ability to create your life exactly as you wish it to be.*** Commit to being 100% accountable and create whatever you desire.

Each moment you must choose
either limitation or expansion, doubt or inspiration.
Your focus activates your consciousness.

The key is activating your potential by focusing on what you want instead of what you don't want! Negative thinking will keep you stuck in survival mode. Shift your focus to create a brand new playing field in your consciousness. You will thrive in every area of your life.

Shifting from surviving to thriving means nurturing your creative energy to GET OUT OF YOUR COMFORT ZONE! Is your inner critic trying to keep you safe in your comfort zone? Awareness is the first step – awareness equals power.

Ask yourself:

- Am I currently "playing it safe"?
- Which restraints or fears are sabotaging my growth?
- Which words and behaviors keep me stuck in survival mode?
- Which three things could I do today to push myself out of my comfort zones?
- Which rewards could I generate by taking this action?

Visualize yourself living your dreams.
Clearly envision yourself taking action and
celebrating your own courage.
Consciously make the decision to BE A
PIONEER IN YOUR OWN LIFE.

Take internal and external action, and don't let the "naysayers" cause you to think small. Have the courage to break new ground, to do things you have never done before. Don't live your life the way other people expect you to. Conforming to other peoples' expectations is a recipe for a humdrum, boring and mediocre life.

To become an authentically wealthy and thriving individual, you must follow the voice of your soul, nurture your own passions, and create your own unique pathway to success. Develop a mindset of abundance by thinking outside the box, by doing what YOUR heart desires. This means thinking and behaving in ways that amplify your self-worth, honor your personal truth, and resonate with your spirit!

Be a pioneer in your own life – walk a new road. Trust your soul to lead you in the direction of your highest potential. It is your life and your path, and no one should create it but you. *Don't be overly concerned about how you look in the eyes of others.* Play the part you create for yourself and never forget YOU choose the way to perceive yourself. Everything else is a reflection of your perception.

Choose your role. Don't let anyone else be in charge of casting the movie of YOUR life! Remember, there is no "wrong" or "right" way for things to turn out. All outcomes are simply experiences, and labeling these experiences is a limitation we should not place on ourselves. To thrive, we must let go. We must create our lives with passion, purpose, confidence and faith. Don't reach the end of your life with regrets! Take action on your passions and dreams now.

It's application time!

Please take out your notebooks and title this exercise:

Clarifying My Soul's Passions.

After some soul- searching, answer the following questions:

- Which activities bring me the most inner excitement and satisfaction?
- What percentage of my time do I devote to these activities? Could I increase this percentage?
- Which experiences have given me the greatest sense of purpose, satisfaction, or accomplishment? (Describe the experiences in detail.)
- When have I felt like I was doing exactly what I was born to do?
- At the end of this life, which dream or passion would cause me the greatest regret for not having pursued it?
- When do I feel most "in the flow?"

When you achieve clarity on your soul's passions, you will feel an immediate surge of energy, vitality, passion and strength surging through you.

> *As you devote more time to nurturing your passions,*
> *incorporating them into your daily life,*
> *you will ignite an enduring sense of enthusiasm.*

You will serve as a magnet for opportunities that will pave the way for financial freedom and success. You will become a beacon of light – attracting the people, situations and opportunities for "soul success".

You will know what it means to THRIVE!

27. Bridging Heaven and Earth

You are an eternal soul living a multidimensional life because multiple dimensions exist simultaneously. Heaven is a different dimension beyond the physical realm and **you can experience the frequencies of "heaven" here on earth.** We think of "heaven" as the place we go when we die – the non-physical dimension we call the after-life. But in truth, **many worlds exist beyond this one, and the afterlife takes many forms.**

Whether we realize it or not, we exist in more than one place at the same time. **The larger non-physical part of us never dies.** It exists in its wholeness just beyond this temporary physical plane we reside in now. We mistakenly believe that these physical bodies are who we are, when the truth is that our bodies are but a fraction of the totality of our essence.

Just because you can't see other dimensions or see the larger non-physical part of yourself, doesn't mean they don't exist.

> *As Carl Sagan brilliantly stated, "Absence of evidence is NOT evidence of absence."*

My own perspective expanded greatly after my near death experience. I have come to realize that on the other side of physical death we merge into the totality of who we are. **Beyond our physical world there is no space and time.** There is a brilliant multidimensional spirit world that exists within us and beyond the confines of this time/space reality.

Each person's heaven is uniquely determined by their consciousness.

On earth, heaven is a "state of being" we experience when we are joyful, loving, compassionate, accepting, harmonious, giving and peaceful. The slower our vibration, the lower our frequency, and so the more closely aligned we are with the state people commonly call "hell." Hell is simply a heavy, dull and dismal state of being, similar to our feelings when we are deeply depressed, self-centered, and vindictive. Hell is not a place we are sent as God's punishment for "bad" deeds. Hell is inside us and it is here and now.

How does this apply to your life? The level of heaven you experience here on earth is self-selected. While in physical form, live with love, gratitude, forgiveness, and harmony to raise your frequency to the highest possible level. Upon physical death, you will re-emerge into the fullness of who you are. While living on earth, your soul is simultaneously dwelling among similar souls in the spiritual realm you will find yourself in after death. ***Your consciousness migrates between an infinite number of dimensions*** because everything exists simultaneously.

> ***You cannot see the multi-dimensional energy levels beyond the physical plane for the same reason you can't see radio or television waves. They exist on frequencies of the light spectrum not visible to our eyes.***

The realms of spiritual energy simply vibrate on higher frequencies. The frequency of love is like heat, which has a higher vibration than colder temperatures. The greater the love, the finer the vibration, and the "closer" we are to "heaven!"

You create a paradise of heaven on earth – within you – when you learn to love and accept yourself as well as others. A change in perception and perspective, is needed to build a bridge between worlds.

> ***You can cross the thresh-hold from the known to the unknown, swim in the divine ocean, and remember your eternal identity without having to shed your physical body!***

Stretch your awareness to remember all you are beyond this physical reality!

You are the universe. You are a gift. As Eckhart Tolle says, "You are not IN the universe, you ARE the universe, an intrinsic part of it. Ultimately you are not a person, but a focal point where the universe is becoming conscious of itself. What an amazing miracle." *Life is the dancer and you are the dance!* You are made from stardust! The unique melody you create and dance to in this life is your personal gift to the whole.

We are all instruments in a universal orchestra, working together on a beautiful and original symphony. *Don't underestimate the gift of your presence and the magnificent role you play in the cosmic symphony.* We are all droplets in a sea of energy, creating ripples as we touch other people before their ripples bounce right back to us. The more you conscious you are of your role, the greater your potential for experiencing "heaven on earth."

Declare inner liberation and experience the ultimate freedom of multi-dimensional living! This is your divine birthright. Create synergy between matter and spirit by expanding your perception and living in awe of the beauty within and around you. Transmute limiting thoughts and beliefs into higher awareness, and integrate greater flexibility, compassion and love into your journey. Ignite the flame of divinity within you! Be a pioneer of multidimensionality!

You bridge heaven and earth by acknowledging that the larger part of you never dies, AND by becoming aware of your creative power.

It also helps to become aware of the soul contracts that you made coming into this lifetime so you can move through them with greater ease. This takes lifetimes of experience and learning, which are mere moments in the vastness of your spiritual curriculum.

As you become aware of the grander purpose of your life, you rise above the heaviness of your challenges. You also raise your spiritual vibration, allowing for greater harmony, peace, joy and love.

> *The universe is a spiritual university, and*
> *earth is just one of the courses.*

You will come to see the bigger picture of each incarnation, including this one. Each incarnation is a hologram where souls rendezvous to complete their soul contracts with one another and further expand through the experiences of "life."

In your divine blueprint, *your soul scheduled essential experiences at specific times and places with other special souls.* These challenges often appear as obstacles, but are actually the greatest facilitators of your expansion and enlightenment. You have the option to complete these prearranged tasks and connections, but not the obligation. Your soul contracts may be short-term or bridge many lifetimes. They are the reasons for your participation on earth, so it's important to see these interactions as opportunities for expansion.

Soul-mate contracts create blissful experiences OR they facilitate emotional triggers for unresolved memories. They reflect all we need to see within ourselves. These contracts come in the form of children, parents, romantic partners, business associates, friends and associates. Each contract brings a gift of heightened awareness.

> *If you wish to bridge heaven and earth to experience the rewards*
> *of your divine potential, take responsibility for the behaviors*
> *which reinforce the repetition of unresolved soul contracts.*

Only then can you complete your divinely prearranged agreements. So, rather than repeatedly clashing with others, notice the divinely designed opportunities for resolution and expansion. Release the battle and step into the flow.

Loving and accepting yourself just as you are is essential to expanding your reality by creating heaven on earth. As you relax into complete self-acceptance, you naturally extend it to others. *All the criticism, judgment, comparison, competition and evaluation fall away when you cultivate self-love.*

It's application time again!

Please take out your notebooks and title this exercise:

30 DAYS TO LOVING MYSELF.

Commit to daily self-nurturing time for 30 consecutive days, and build your very own bridge between worlds. As you practice loving and accepting yourself just as you are, you will merge with your eternal identity a little more each day. You will become a beacon of light, an example of heaven on earth being created from within.

This daily exercise includes the combination of the "**I AM LOVE**" **Self-Nurturing Meditation and the "I AM POWERFUL BEYOND MEASURE**" affirmation.

Please note your begin and end dates.

Commit to nurturing your infinite potential and honoring your soul by doing this meditation every day for 30 days.

It's simple, quick and powerful, and holds keys that will generate miracles within you and around you. Heaven on earth will enter your relationships, career, finances, health and well being. And it only takes a matter of minutes each day. Your dedication to unconditional self love and acceptance will produce transformative results, and *your life will shift from ordinary to extraordinary!*

Cari L. Murphy

"I AM LOVE" MEDITATION:

Step 1: Place your hands over your heart and gently close your eyes.

Step 2: Repeat the following statement ten times, either out loud or silently:

"I AM LOVE. I LOVE MYSELF JUST AS I AM."

Imagine you are connecting with your Divine Self – expanding the brilliant light, the magnificent radiance of the unconditional love of your eternal self. Exult in your magnificence and allow the divine light to saturate your consciousness gracefully, powerfully and easily.

"I AM POWERFUL" AFFIRMATION

"I AM" may be two small words, but they are still the most powerful words in the world. The "I AM" proclamation generates powerful and positive shifts in your spirit.

> *Embrace the truth of who you are by stating your "I Am" affirmation each day for 30 days, helping you merge your soul's magnificence with your human ego/personality.*

As you affirm these "I AM" statements, you will gradually remember your true self as you manifest miracles in your life. You will feel and experience the results of this truth all around you.

Each day for thirty days, affirm the loving soul you already are, and come to possess true power as an infinite and limitlessly creative being.

"I AM POWERFUL" Affirmation: Day 1

★With your hands on your heart, repeat the initial "I AM LOVE" meditation ten times and **follow it up with the "I Am"affirmation of the day.**

So, day #1 would consist of this brief love meditation : "I AM LOVE. I LOVE MYSELF JUST AS I AM. " FOLLOW UP WITH ONE OF THE AFFIRMATIONS BELOW:

- ⚔ "I am important and I cherish my unique presence."
- ⚔ "I am bathed in the infinite light of love. I celebrate and cherish my gifts."
- ⚔ "I am valued, treasured, and acknowledged in all my relation-ships. I create balance and harmony wherever I go."

Your intention and openness, coupled with shifting your perception, will actually change your surroundings. You are your very own universe of swirling subatomic particles, and a simple shift in your perspective will powerfully change the formations of these particles, creating a new reality for you. Build a bridge between worlds to blend your energy field with the cosmos. *Cultivate your multidimensionality* by visualizing yourself merging into the infinite stream of life.

Don't underestimate the value of your life and the gift of your presence!

> *You are an instrument of the divine,*
> *composing your own cosmic symphonies here on earth.*

Feel the magic within and around you by visualizing yourself floating amongst the stardust – shimmering brightly as you shine your light on all around you.

Transform your daily existence from the dull and ordinary to the vibrant and extraordinary!

Delight in your liberation.

Your soul is sending you a divine invitation. Will you accept it?

28. Generating Momentum

If momentum is always being generated, how does it happen? We generate momentum by actively focusing our attention. *The key is to be aware of the type of momentum we generate,* with a goal of creating a deliberate, steady stream of positive momentum.

We pave the way for infinitely successful tomorrows with today's positive thoughts, feelings, actions and responses.

Each moment offers choice, so we consciously (or subconsciously) choose limitation or expansion, doubt or inspiration many times each day. Joy, Laughter, Spontaneity, Appreciation, Playfulness, Inspiration and Passion are self-selected, high-frequency emotions that generate positive momentum to support our inspiration and expansion.

The focus of your power is always in the present, so choose to purposefully create momentum in your life. Begin with a personal commitment to create an *exceptionally successful mindset*.

Broadcast a bright, positive vibration into the world and you're bound to attract brilliant results!

Every outcome in your life results from the vibrational signals you transmit, so step into the playground of infinite possibility and potential by realizing you are the sole creator of your experiences.

Remember, *the journey is the joy!*
There is no finish line because you are eternal!

Add your own color, shine and vibrancy to each day by generating your own momentum. Don't wait for the world around you to determine your mood and its resulting frequency. Enjoy the game of life beause there are no "winners" or "losers". There are simply people who play consciously and those who drift on auto-pilot. It's so much more fun to play deliberately, with focus and awareness.

Have as much fun as possible each day and don't wait to celebrate! Celebrate now. Never wait for your "luck" to turn before celebrating.

The real secret to success is celebrating first and allowing that positive momentum to attract circumstances calling for a celebration!

There are no accidents, just response to your vibrational output. No exceptions. This may be hard to accept when things aren't going your way, but it's the most liberating piece of information you'll ever hear. You always have the power to adjust your vibration to change your results.

Feel the joy, passion, and exhilaration from creating your moment-to-moment experiences with the power of your focus! Be playful instead of urgent and have fun with your creative ability. Don't try so hard! Fear-based urgency interrupts the flow of inspired action, and only inspired action generates lasting success. Action rooted in fear results in fleeting success at best. Recognize the value of your focus and stop trying to control or resist your experience. You will SOAR. Refrain from analyzing, judging, defending or explaining yourself. Those are sure-fire signs of resistance, the kind of contradictory energy that blocks the path to the fulfillment of your desires. You cannot resist and receive at the same time! Hold a thought or idea without contradictory energy, and you will generate the positive momentum to reach your goal.

Bottom line: Reduce resistance and increase allowance and get ready for pure inspiration!

Enjoy your role as a conscious, joyful creator.
Don't postpone your bliss by waiting for
someone else to bring it into your life!

Claim it NOW and enjoy positive anticipation, enthusiasm and happiness as often as possible. Only you can give yourself this energy boost! It is always available. *Study your vibrations and choose only the ones that generate positive results.*

What kind of momentum are YOU currently generating? To answer this you must first answer the following question about your focus: It your focus geared to criticize or praise your current experience? Your answer will determine what's coming next!

Others will rise to meet your dominant expectation of them, so choose to praise others more often! See others as you wish to see yourself. Look for things to appreciate and praise. To generate positive momentum, focus your attention on what you want to experience MORE of. As you consistently do this, you will experience new, more successful results.

Life is far simpler than we make it. *We can choose to feel a little better or a little worse in every moment.* **We increase the quality of our lives by creating momentum to move toward a better feeling than the one we're currently experiencing.** If generating momentum based on feelings of exhilaration or enthusiasm seems out of reach to you, simply exercise your power to feel a little better than you did yesterday. Recognize your ability to amplify feelings of generalized appreciation instead of feelings of frustration or discontent directed at specific events. *Let go of the tension associated with your resistance.*

Present choices create future experiences, so focus your attention on anything and everything that brings you satisfaction and peace.

Step into the flow by amplifying these vibrations. Arrest the downward momentum and create an upward spiral of momentum to allow greater blessings to flow into your experience. Focus selectively, radiate positive energy, and step into your power!

Refine your vibrations by sifting through all the old patterns of negative momentum and cycles of discontent.

> *Remember, focusing your attention on something*
> *is your personal invitation to bring its presence in your experience.*

So, create momentum that supports your success by ignoring what's bothering you and emphasizing all that's going well in your life.

Deliberately tune out any circumstance or person who is not in tune with your aspirations for health, wealth and harmony! Stop going counter to the direction your soul wants you to go, and you will feel relief! Imagine driving 75 mph on the freeway when you notice a wreck ahead and slow down to 0 mph. As soon as the roadway clears, traffic picks up again. You're not back to 75 mph right away, but going 15 mph feels really good! You can do this in your life by letting go of emotional resistance and stepping into the positive flow.

Shift your vibrational output to a signal that attracts opportunity, and you will transform your life – from the inside-out.

It's application time again!

Please take out your notebooks and title this exercise:

<u>My Positive Momentum Journal</u>

Consistent positive momentum comes from consciously focusing on what's working in your life. You could devote an entire notebook to this exercise alone.

Set time aside each day to acknowledge
all the people and experiences currently working for you.

Place your attention on all the ways your life is "working", and fuel your expansion with the power of self-generated momentum!

The key is writing in your momentum journal daily.
Commit to doing it for thirty days.

Commit to reaching for resonance with your desires and dreams. At the end of that period, look back on all the successes you've recounted in your journal! We often forget to notice **what powerful magnets we are!** Take note of the positive people and situations you attract into your experience on a daily basis, and feel inspired to to reach for even greater success for yourself: Own your focus and use it to generate happiness and prosperity beyond your wildest dreams.

As you commit to focusing on feelings that generate positive momentum, reality will change to match your new vibration! Achievement comes on the heels of consistently held vibrations, so select yours deliberately and nothing will be off limits to you!

Remember, **the universe always matches your "now signal." So, as this signal changes, so does your reality.** Your vibrational output can shift from moment to moment, so it doesn't matter what you created in the past. Each day begins with a blank slate awaiting your new vibration, a vibration that will determine your outcomes for the day! Each moment, you activate limitation or expansion, separation or connection. Choose expansion and connection! Actively select the tone that will yield the most beneficial outcomes in your life.

Don't allow anyone or anything outside you to set your tone.
BE YOUR OWN DAILY TONE-SETTER!
There is nothing more empowering than that.

How you feel is a powerful indicator of the signal you are broadcasting, so practice new, successful signals on a daily basis. You will ***reap the rewards of deliberately selecting a positive signal*** because you will notice the universe matching it with a positive external reality! Get a rhythm going in your life that feels great!

Consistently shine the spotlight on your strengths and see the result of those strengths in the opportunities that easily come your way. There's nothing better than realizing your power as the conscious creator of your life.

> ***Once you experience the delicious results of living this way, you'll never go back to auto-pilot living again!***

29. FROM STRESSED TO BLESSED

Do you ever feel like giving up on the life of your dreams because it seems to take every ounce of energy just to make it through each day? Within you is a power so profound it will help you view stress as an ally instead of the enemy.

> *Stress, from a broader perspective, is a gift – from your body – revealing the need for change.*

Beginning today, start a new habit of interpreting stressful moments as opportunities for greater authenticity and expansion. Then, your experiences will flow with grace and ease and you will be astonished by your ability to **navigate life as an infinitely powerful creator.**

The true measure of success is happiness. Our primary goal in life is to be happy. So, identify the people, experiences and environments that bring you joy, and remain focused in those directions. When you know your destination, the journey becomes harmonious, the twists and turns fluid. You will change from being stressed to being blessed.

Claim control of your experiences to live a blessed life. Become energetically invincible, so nothing holds the power to push you "off center." Zero in on the points of attraction that generate feelings of ease, wellness and harmony, so **your magnetism begins to work for you instead of against you.** People respond to your energy, so control the vibrations you send out! Consciously choose what to attract into your life, as well as what to repel.

A stressed life leads to stagnation, while a blessed one leads to expansion. Stress is the result of misdirected focus. When we focus on what is "missing" or on what's "wrong", we amplify stress levels by binding ourselves to our present circumstances. We must shift focus to **pay attention to what we want to experience instead of zeroing in on what is "lacking" in our lives.**

There is no such thing as "fixing" a problem! We only compound them with our attention.

> **We reduce stress by being solution-oriented**
> **instead of problem-oriented.**

Solutions can't be found on the same frequency as problems because the signals are different. You might as well look for classical music on a heavy metal radio station. Focus your energy on the higher frequencies where solutions are created by emitting vibrations that attract the people and experiences that will create the life you desire. Your "problems" will melt away as a result.

Any time we feel we must justify our beliefs, we step out of the flow. When we truly know or believe something, we don't have to "prove it." The need to sway or convince others creates a strong vibration of doubt in our energy fields, countering the positive vibration of our belief. **We cannot resist and receive at the same time!**

We must keep our attention OFF topics that create discord and ON topics that allow us to create new and better experiences. **We cannot reach our goals by creating roadblocks** which sabotage our expansion. We must clear the pathway to allow an unlimited flow of blessings into our lives.

How? Anytime we find ourselves talking about what we don't want, simply shift focus to what we DO want and how we DO want to feel!

> **Chaos, distress and frustration typically comes**
> **from re-hashing experiences that have generated discord in the past.**

Freedom is realizing we have choices. We can choose to relive the same old stories or create new ones reflecting the lives we wish to experience.

The direction of our focus generates the momentum for feeling stressed or blessed. Choose statements that place you on a **direct pathway to the outcomes you most desire,** statements that will generate positive momentum. Become pro-active with your focus instead of reacting to the people and situations you should eliminate from your life. Stop wasting your energy trying to get rid of what you don't want and focus on what you do want! Give your undivided attention to creating experiences that generate happiness in your life!

You can rise above your challenges and their associated stress by simply ignoring them! Instead, lean in directions that bring peace into your life. **You can't make progress by looking backward! Expansion occurs when we look ahead to shine a spotlight on new possibilities.** So, deactivate the thoughts, feelings and expectations that hinder your progress, and simply focus on what you want!

Elevate your vibration to reflect your dreams instead of your worries. Train yourself to transmit vibrations which attracts all things positive! Establish new patterns of thoughts and actions to attract further blessings in your life! **Focus less on what you don't want and more on what you DO want, and blessings will flow** naturally into your day-to-day experiences.

It's time to jump-start your bliss! When you're stressed, you forfeit your creative ability by moving to the passenger's seat and allowing your circumstances to steer your life. **Claim your creative power by putting yourself back in the driver's seat and taking full responsibility for navigating the pathway of your life.**

Too often we live in old, familiar spaces where stress and discomfort feel normal! Some of us have resided there so long that emotional and physical exhaustion have become our default mode of living. We've accepted burnout as our life sentence. It's time to reset your default mode!

How often do you install a new computer program and click the default tab instead of customizing it? We all do it, right? *We don't want to spend the time learning something new so we choose the default icon.*

⚔ What about YOUR inner world?
⚔ Are you living your life by DEFAULT?
⚔ Are you just going through the motions of everyday life the way you've been trained to do?
⚔ How often do you wish your life were better or different?
⚔ When you see others succeeding in ways you are not, don't you wish you could do the same?

You have two choices in life.
You can live by default AND select the default button
OR you can listen to the voice of your soul
urging you to click on the customize button instead!

You must think outside the box to evolve from stressed to blessed living! Simply making the leap of faith to push the customize tab is a powerful first step. There is no need to settle for a mundane life set on auto-pilot where others make choices for you. Let go of what others think is the best customizable approach for your life. Customize your experiences by refining your preferences and identifying what you desire. *Get comfortable clarifying your dreams and say to yourself, "THIS is how I want things to be"!*

You can retrain yourself moment by moment and day to day. *Shift into conscious creator mode in your new Empowered Life!* Practice and have fun with it! Learn to customize your life until you feel your inner voice **SMILE**.

It's time to trade your limited reality for one more empowering and rewarding! It's time to change your vibrational ZIP code and activate your personal power. Clarify the ways you sabotage yourself and *acknowledge your most consistent patterns of criticism and praise with the following exercise.*

This will help you release the stress, discontent and chaos in your life.

It's application time!

Please take out your notebooks and title this exercise:

CRITICISM OR PRAISE

At the top of your page, make a list with the following headers:

- **MYSELF**
- **MY LOVED ONES**
- **MY ENVIRONMENT**
- **MY JOB/COLLEAGES/CLIENTS**

Spend a day listing the subjects your criticize or praise most consistently. This will sharpen awareness about the sources of stress and blessings in your life. Then, *shift your focus to praise more often and criticize LESS OFTEN, and watch the improved quality of the experiences you attract.*

You deserve a life filled with blessings – *an easy and fluid lifestyle.* Discipline your focus, send out consistently positive vibrations that resonate with your true self. You will naturally rise above struggle and into alignment with the success you desire and deserve. Claim the benefits of your creative control.

Stop struggling with stressful subjects and people. Release the problems and negativity, and refocus your energy in beneficial directions.

Rest assured you will see powerful, positive results in your day-to-day experiences.

Prepare for a life free from stress and overflowing with blessings.

This is your birthright!

30. Enjoy the Ride

This book contains insights of divine design which I hope will provide clarity and inspiration on your soul's journey. These "treasures from heaven" are wonderful lessons about **consciously creating your life's masterpiece with grace and ease.**

> *Everything in these pages is meant to support your contribution to the cosmic symphony.*

My deepest desire is for you to continue progressing through your soul's divine blueprint. Every page in this book is a simple reminder of the eternal wisdom already contained within you. **Remember your life is a gift.** You are a gift, not simply an "opportunity." Seeing life as an opportunity would imply success or failure, but your soul sees only an experience. Live consciously and revel in your multidimensional nature, propel yourself beyond success and failure, into the purity and perfection of simply "being."

Your reward is liberation. Appreciate your experiences without clinging to them. The present moment is all that exists, so make each moment the primary focus of your life! Your unique life is the spiritual universe expressing itself in physical form. Enjoy your creative power during your journey.

> *You are the play and the player,*
> *the producer and the director,*
> *as well as the audience.*
> *Don't act out someone else's production*
> *or allow someone else to write your script!*

You wrote much of this life's script before you were born, so you are free to choose the richness and depth of your experience. Don't focus too long on the frustrations that accompany your divinely designed challenges.

You decide the height of the "highs" and the depth of the "lows."

You choose your perspective,
so view your life through divinely-colored glasses,
and live the dream.

You are an eternal being. The reasons you choose to walk this particular path, with all its dramas and traumas, is beyond human understanding. But spiritually, the puzzle of your divine blueprint comes together piece by piece, to form a beautiful and magnificent cosmic tapestry. Your struggles are important, but don't judge yourself by them. Receive your challenges as opportunities to make your life as fun and interesting as possible! Take chances and live your dreams.

BE YOURSELF, and as light-hearted as often as possible. Don't take yourself too seriously! Accept yourself completely for who you are at this moment. Even if you feel fear, accept it. It will pass. Don't judge yourself or shy away from feeling fear. Accept it. Only by accepting fear and allowing it to pass will you transcend it. The more you try to control things, the more you get caught up in self-created drama.

Whatever your challenges,
wherever you are in your life, trust that "this too shall pass."

You must accept your present before you can move forward. The more fully you accept yourself in your current circumstances, the easier life will flow, and the easier it will be to accept others. Focus on the present, and don't spend your precious time worrying about the future! Be at peace with where you are now and do what brings you joy.

Simplify your life instead of complicating your journey.

You are meant to enjoy life.

You are intended to have FUN *and* **EXPAND** at the same time!

Thank you for taking this walk with me.

May your path be filled with infinite wonder and delight...

About the Author

Cari Murphy is an World Renowned Media Host, Business and Success Coach coaching tens of thousands globally, Inspirational Speaker, and Award Winning Spiritual Author of 5 Books, including the Best-Seller *Create Change Now*. As the Host the of the Internationally Syndicated Radio Program *"THE CARI MURPHY SHOW: STRAIGHT TALK FOR THE SOUL"* with almost one million listeners (named "Best Spiritual Radio Show for 2013), the President and CEO of Empowerment Coaching Solutions and a regularly featured seminar presenter, Cari is dedicated to empowering millions globally. Following a near death experience in 1997, Cari's purpose became clear. She is passionately devoted to empowering her clients, audiences, and readers to shift from dull, uninspired, auto-pilot living into purposeful living, unleash their greatest potential, and claim the inner worth, outer wealth, and optimal health they desire and deserve.

Website: www.CariMurphy.com
Contact Cari Toll-Free at 1-800-704-SOUL